THE UNITED STATES IN PROPHESY

AMERICA GLOBALISM AND THE FALSE PROPHET

Ken Klein

Winterhaven Publishing House
Eugene, Oregon 97401

Scripture quotations are taken from the King James Version of the Bible.

Contents

Preface

From time to time, men should be unafraid to shake up their thinking. Why do we do what we do? Why do we think what we think? For some this could be an intimidating exercise. Some say, "Whatever can be shaken will be shaken." But if we are really standing on the Rock, we should fearlessly embrace the challenge. After all, who wants to build on sand?

The teachings presented in this book challenge the fundamental Christian worldview and, on a grander scale, call into serious question today's predominant biblical eschatological (prophetic) point of view.

The initial launching pad is the premise that *there has never been a clear guidance system for the interpretation of the book of Revelation.* The Christian community has had only a vague understanding of John's Revelation because the context of the Revelation has *never* been pinpointed with clear biblical clarity. Once the context has been grasped then sound interpretation can follow. Herein lies the clarity.

THE CONTEXT

First, the letter is from Him who *is*, who *was*, and who *is to come* (Revelation 1:4). God, who *is*, lives in the realm of eternity; He is. He *was*, meaning He, Jesus, was amongst men when He died (on the cross). He *is to come*; He will return to this time dimension at His Second Coming. We see this explanation of God's existence from heaven to earth. He *is*, He *was*, He *is to come*. We also see that the letter was written from the presence of the seven spirits before the throne of God. The context of the writing is heaven and eternity.

5

Second, He is the Alpha and the Omega (Revelation 1:8), the beginning and the end. This verse speaks of time as we know it; God, who is, has no beginning nor end. He is from the beginning of creation until the end of time as we presently know it. In other words, God is outside of time, and He sees time from the end to the beginning and from the beginning to the end—all at once.

In order for us to wrap our minds around the true meaning of the symbols of Revelation, we must begin by grasping the context of the writings of Revelation. The context is written from outside of time as we know it.

This is an enormous problem. Our minds naturally operate within the context of human time. We are programmed to think and conceptualize within the context of historical time. In the book of Revelation, we are faced with trying to understand matters from outside of time—from God's point of view. If we do not begin with this premise, we tend to force a materialization of application (an earthly meaning) on the symbols before we understand their spiritual nature and meaning.

Third, John says, "I was in the spirit on the Lord's day" (Revelation 1:10). Does anyone really know what this means?

Perhaps the apostle Paul did. He informs us of a man (himself) who was caught up; whether he was in the body or not he couldn't say (2 Corinthians 10:2). He was lifted out of time, as was John when he received the Revelation.

Peter also may have been able to tell us. He fell into a trance while sitting on a rooftop and saw a sheet descending with unclean animals. "What I have cleansed no longer treat as unclean," God said to Peter. But the Lord's command—"Arise, Peter, kill and eat"—had nothing to do with eating unclean animals. It had to do with how God was accepting the Gentiles. The symbol of the sheet and the unclean animals had nothing to do with the tangible eating of unclean flesh as Peter initially thought. It was about a spiritual matter. Salvation was being opened up to the Gentiles.

When Peter, James, and John accompanied Jesus to the Mount of Transfiguration they were transported into the realm of the "spirit" and became terrified. Notice what they said: "Let us make three tabernacles, Lord. One for you, one for Moses, and one for Elijah." They were trying to bring their spiritual experience into an earthly time context. This is exactly the problem with our approach to the book of Revelation. *We try to recontextualize the book according to time as we know it.*

This problem becomes more prominently evidenced in modern teachings. Revelation 1:19 says, "Write the things which thou hast seen, and the things which are, and the things which shall be hereafter." Immediately we assume that this means past, present, and future—earth time. We force the interpretation into an earthly time sequence. But the context is not earth time. It is heaven time. He is seeing these things in the spirit, not on the earth. The sequence of the heavenly events are just that: in heaven.

The book of Revelation is about spiritual codes that are written in symbolic form or language and unfolded in a certain sequence: Things that he has already seen, things that he is about to see, and things that he will see in the "spirit." Most of our thinking about Revelation has been misplaced into earth time chronology.

Since all appropriate biblical exegeses utilize the principle of time (the eternal Word was spoken in time), history is an essential element for interpretation of Scripture. *But the book of Revelation has no earthly historical context.* It is written from a heavenly perspective.

Man's problem in attempting to interpret the Revelation is that he is trapped in time, causing him to invent a historical (earthly) perspective. *Proper context is the key to understanding the most mystical book ever written.* It was written from God's view point, God's context, outside of time as we know it.

Introduction

In a large office sequestered in a small English town, a man sits in front of an enormous but primitive computer system. With his headphones on, he strains to listen. The year is 1941; the town, Blachly Park. The office is British counterintelligence for Europe. The computer is the newly constructed cipher system, eavesdropping on the German military broadcasts. The German code: the enigma.

Over the past number of years, television's history channels have effectively reported on some of the greatest secrets of World War II. England's brilliant de-encrypting technology via the invention of the computer cipher was the most important weapon of the allies in World War II. The brain trust that created the cipher was the greatest assembly of talent of the war. Although Germany had suspicions they were being spied on, they never figured it out.

Hitler and the German high command did not believe it was possible that the enigma code could be cracked. It was much too complicated. Nonetheless, the Führer took precautions by scrambling the code on a daily basis. Yet, British intelligence was still able to consistently intercept information from Hitler's Third Reich. As a result of this tremendous advantage, the Allies were able to continuously outflank the German wolf packs (submarines) in the north Atlantic. Not only was the battle for the Atlantic successful, but the Allies' advance information continually frustrated German strategy and tactics in the land battles for Europe as well.

But then it happened. A high-ranking officer of the German military carried a bomb in a briefcase into a secret meeting with Hitler. The bomb was placed at the feet of the Führer. The bomb exploded, and Hitler was seriously wounded. The assassination attempt failed. Hitler survived. The war continued. But the attempt on his life made him exceedingly paranoid. He refused to allow any war-related information to be communicated by radio. All information was passed by couriers, who were guarded by his infamous and trusted Gestapo.

Back at Blachly Park, message interception—and, thus, the flow of secretly deciphered information—screeched to a halt. An intelligence blackout. For the first time since America's entry into the war, the Allies were blind. They had become so dependent on this rich source of intercepted German information that the intelligence blackout led to the greatest military blunder in all history.

Three months after the blackout, the Allies were confident that Germany was defeated in that late summer of 1944. However, without upgraded information on the state of the German war planning, they were headed into a grave error. They fell into a state of optimism and complacency, falsely believing the war was coming to an end. After all, France was being liberated, and the German army was retreating back to their own borders.

But Hitler had a secret plan: "The Waht on the Rhine," a massive military counteroffensive. Better known today as the "Battle of the Bulge," it was a massive military operation that came seriously close to succeeding.

Heroic men saved the day, and Germany's last gasp did not succeed. Had it succeeded, Hitler would have gained atomic weaponry, and the world would be a far different place today.

What a lesson! But what can we learn from it?

Have we lost our ability to cipher prophetic events in the light of biblical prophecy? Has a massive satanic counteroffensive been launched against God's kingdom and we have become overly confident—like the Allied generals of World War II? Are we aware of what is taking place, or have we become dulled down to the degree that we cannot see what is really happening? What has become of our objective perspective? And how does America fit into the end time scenario.

These are the questions that will be addressed and answered in this book.

CHAPTER ONE

The Last Stroke

They slipped out of New York without being seen.

They changed their names and rode the lowly subways. They falsified their itinerary. In the middle of the night they made their way to the secret meeting place.

Their rendezvous had been carefully prepared. Already, the hideaway was sealed off and guarded in strictest isolation. All English-speaking servants were released. Every possible leak of information was sealed. There was no chance for knowledge of the event taking place to slip out. What was at hand was the final episode in the conquest of the United States of America, the event that would consummate a two-hundred-year plot to seize the hidden conduits of international capital.

This last stroke, the final blow, would affect the realization of an ancient conspiracy that would finance a new Global World

Empire. The means would be the centralization and control of money.

The secret location for the meeting was a millionaire's retreat called Jekyll Island, located off the coast of Georgia.[1] No name could have been more fitting for such a place of treachery.

The name Jekyll was immortalized by the great American author Robert Lewis Stevenson in his famous book *Dr. Jekyll and Mr. Hyde*. Stevenson's masterpiece tells the story of a benevolent Dr. Jekyll, who, while working in his laboratory, discovers a drug that turns him into a beast (Mr. Hyde).

Jekyll Island, a place of seclusion and tranquillity owned by the rich and powerful, became a laboratory for concocting an evil scheme. The potion of this scheme, once consumed by the American republic, transformed it into a Mr. Hyde, a beast.[2] This is the true story of six thousand years of watching and waiting for the final rebellion, characterized by the emergence of a Global World Government of promised peace and prosperity.

The last two centuries have witnessed the final chiseling of an ancient historic monument—a monument erected by the corporate will of the human race. There is an inscription at the foot of the edifice revealing a fantastic testimonial: *Man without God is a beast.*

THE CHOSEN ONES

For hundreds of years the people of God have been anticipating a Global World Empire ruled by the Antichrist. In the 1930s and 1940s, many thought that Adolf Hitler and Benito Mussolini were the Antichrist and the False Prophet. Bible believers viewed the National Socialist German Worker's (Nazi) party as the Beast that would fulfill the prophecy of Daniel and Revelation. In the 1960s, scholars and spokesmen from Dallas Theological Seminary, and books such as Hal Lindsay's *The Late Great Planet Earth*, focused the North American church, both Protestant and Roman Catholic, on the European continent as the place where the Beast would rise with his ten horns or kings.[3]

When it became known that the European Common Market would be limited to ten nations, it seemed clear to many that those nations comprised the ten kings. It looked as though the European nations perfectly fit into the fulfillment of Daniel's and John's prophecies.

A horn in Scripture is interpreted as a king or a kingdom, so the announcement created much interest and excitement in the church world. However, now there are more than ten members of the Common Market, and after many years the excitement has waned.

As a result, many today are perplexed and confused trying to figure out how all the prophecies fit together.

The European Common Market has now grown well beyond ten nations with several Eastern European nations joining, but Scripture is clear that there will be ten kings that are submitted to the little horn, the Antichrist. During the Nixon administration, the United States was divided into ten economic zones. In addition, the Club of Rome announced that the world globe has been divided into ten federated economic regions. Which of these scenarios represents the mysterious ten kings? The fact of the matter is that the mysterious ten kings have yet to clearly materialize, but, according to Scripture, they will.

But how will this come about? Who and what are driving the world toward this World Global Empire? What role did these powerful men gathered at Jekyll Island play in the formation of this anticipated Global Empire?

THE INSTRUMENTS OF DARKNESS

From the time of man's expulsion by the Lord from the Garden of Eden, history has recorded the efforts of the "god of this world" (Satan) and his relentless movements to consolidate and control this planet. The notion that a man can be righteous in and of himself without spiritual rebirth is the annoying but pervasive sound played on the flute of hell's Pied Piper. For some six thousand years, the children of Adam have danced to that tune, but the song is about to end.

Through powerful spiritual forces working behind the scenes of the visible world, over the millennia man has dutifully and collectively—and blindly—worked on earth to bring about the final rebellion against God in this neo-Babylon called the New World Global Order.

There are some men, to be sure, who have taken actual oaths to the devil himself, and knowingly set themselves to do battle against God. Others have unwittingly become ensnared in the plot. But in this conflict there is no middle ground; one is either for or against the Lord. In the realm of the spirit, the battle lines have been drawn, and very soon the mark of the Beast will be the line drawn in the earth. Whoever takes that mark will have no hope.

From Nimrod to Caesar, from Weishaupt to Hitler, and, ultimately, to the Antichrist himself, the events of history have been, and are being, orchestrated toward a One World Government and the worship of a man—the Antichrist, who will one day proclaim himself to be king of the world.

Through technology, religion, politics, and money, the world has been duped, and we are moving ever closer to that day.

Now, as the cornerstone of the Global World Order has been laid, the nations of the world are unaware of the terrible iron trap that is about to snap closed. Where are "the sons of light"? Where are the prophets—the Daniels, the Jonahs, the Jeremiahs? Who will declare this age?

CHAPTER TWO

The Brothers

Except a corn of wheat fall into the ground and die, it
abideth alone: but if it die, it bringeth forth much fruit.

John 12:24

So begins one of the greatest Russian novels of all time, *The Brothers Karamazov* by Dostoevsky. Dostoevsky was concerned about man's conscience and his responsibility for his brother. This theme ripples through his book.

The question, "Am I my brother's keeper?" is best addressed in the book of Genesis. At the dawn of history, Adam and Eve, the progenitors of the entire human race, gave birth to two sons. They named them Cain and Abel. The lives of these brothers, though real, are also symbolic in nature and represent two great spiritual truths. A careful analysis of them will explain the forces that have worked down through time shaping the whole of human history.

Cain was a farmer, a tiller of the soil. Abel was a shepherd. When the time came to worship God (Genesis 4:3,4), Cain offered the fruit of the ground. Abel took one of the first born of his flock and slew it before the Lord. According to Scripture, Abel's offering was accepted by God while Cain's was rejected.

The question naturally arises, why did God accept Abel's offering and reject Cain's? A close inspection of each man's approach to God will reveal the role of the two principles of life which emanate from these brothers and flow like rivers through the course of human history. These principles affect the governing of the human conscience—and, therefore, affect every human being ever born. In Abel we see the "Mystery of Righteousness," and in Cain the "Mystery of Iniquity."

THE TWO MYSTERIOUS TREES

The Mystery of Righteousness corresponds to the tree of life, which we find in the garden of Eden. The Mystery of Righteousness was the life of God, the tree from which man was allowed to partake freely when he lived in the original state God had intended. The life of God is eternal life. As long as man ate of that tree he would live forever.

In the garden God placed another tree. This was the tree of the knowledge of good and evil. But of this tree God commanded man not to partake. This second tree created a dilemma. Through this dilemma, God established man as a sovereign entity by giving him the opportunity to exercise choice. Man could choose to continue to partake of the tree of eternal life, or he could choose to partake of the tree of the knowledge of good and evil.

There was another consideration attached to the exercising of choice: God said regarding the tree of the knowledge of good and evil, "in the day that you eatest thereof thou shalt surely die" (Genesis 2:17). There was a dire consequence for disobeying God's directive. Notice that the tree gave the knowledge of both good and evil, not just evil. What in actuality was this tree of the knowledge of good and evil?

The tree of the knowledge of good and evil represented the Law. In the Mosaic Law the commandment "Thou shalt not steal" (Exodus 20:15) established the fact that stealing is contrary to God's righteous nature. On the other hand, the Law also implied the opposite. That is, to not steal is an act of righteousness.

Here is a demonstration of the knowledge of good and evil as defined by the Law that separates good and evil. Eating the fruit in disobedience to God had terrible consequences. Not only did breaking God's Law mean death, it meant that one was all the more bound by the Law. The rule of law simply served to show how far man had fallen from God's nature. While the life of God manifest in the "tree of life" could produce righteousness, the tree of the knowledge of good and evil could not. The tree of the knowledge of good and evil was a curse: It gave a knowledge of righteousness because it could divide between good and evil, but it could not produce righteousness. There was no empowering.

The partaking of the tree of the knowledge of good and evil produced the fruit of death; hence, to this day, all men must die. Consequently, the deadly fruit reaped by Adam and Eve has overtaken the entire human race from the beginning of time. All humanity has been born under the Law—under the curse of the tree of the knowledge of good and evil.

THE MYSTERY OF RIGHTEOUSNESS

The Tree of Life

When Abel took a lamb and sacrificed it to God, his act of worship demonstrated a recognition and fundamental understanding of the human predicament. Abel saw himself defiled and separated from a holy God with no means of restoration. In humility Abel came before God, acknowledging his need for cleansing and forgiveness. He recognized that it was humanly impossible to regain the former estate and be released from judgment. By himself it was a hopeless proposition. As a result of this understanding, he made his appeal to God—and hoped that He was merciful.

Abel's recognition of his own depravity and hopeless condition was key for him to make the acceptable and appropriate sacrifice. Though the written Law did not come until Moses, centuries later, Abel knew the truth because the Law was written on his heart—as it is with all men. He recognized that his fallen nature would continually fall short of God's perfect standard. No matter how sincere and consistent his efforts to conform to righteousness, he was trapped in his fallen nature; a slave to his inability to live the Law perfectly. It is the same with all men.

Abel's sacrifice to God was not a representation of his own labor or ability. On the contrary, it was a representation of his recognition that no work or human effort could gain him the approval and acceptance of God for a restored relationship. God, in His mercy, accepted Abel's sacrifice because it was an offering based upon his need, not his effort.

In Abel's sacrifice we have a preview of the Messianic purpose of Jesus, who is, in Himself, the sacrifice. Christ fulfilled the requirements of the Law. He was the perfect sacrifice, which Abel's sacrifice foreshadowed and foretold.

CAINISM

The recognition of iniquity comes from the knowledge of the Law, for the Law explains good and evil. The greater the knowledge, the more profound the effect upon the conscience. This was Cain's irreconcilable predicament.

Cain's worship offering to God was essentially a representation of the work of his hands, his own effort. Cain sought approval and relationship with God on the basis of his own effort: his hard work. He was the embodiment of today's self-made man.

Cain's understanding represents the antithesis of Abel's, and it is characteristic of the same delusion that has always rested on the mass of humanity. Tragically, Cain never arrived at the awareness of his untenable situation. He tried to atone by works, and God refused his sacrifice. His futile attempt to connect with God was not based upon a recognition of his predicament and his need. Consequently, his sacrifice was rejected (Genesis 4:57).

In each man's sacrificial approach to God his thought life was radically set in motion. Cain's approach brought rejection;

hence, anger, hatred, and murder filled his heart. Abel's approach brought acceptance with God, and peace reigned in his heart and mind.

The conscience is the doorway through which thought enters the great room of consciousness. Human thought correspondingly produces behavior. Thus conscience, whether based upon proper or improper relationship with God, affects the thought life and, subsequently, behavior. This is why the thought life needs to be grounded in sound doctrine from Scripture.

This principle of human action as the outworking of conscience not only applies to individuals singularly but also to corporate bodies, in the collective conscience of a group (or even of a nation or state). An example of this on a group level would be the vigilantism of a mob lynching. The mob, trying to right a perceived wrong, collectively commits the sin of Cain (i.e., murder). The same corporate confusion applies in a riot.

Grasping the critical lesson of the story of Cain calls for great objectivity. But if we can wrap our minds around this curious story we can observe the impact of these principles on the whole of human history. Since the principles are dynamic, and not static, failure to grasp the importance of the story results in a vulnerability to deception by the spiritual forces that operate unseen—forces that weaken the Christian worldview.

Cain and the Christian Worldview

Cainism has weakened the Christian worldview throughout time. It is man's approach to God on the basis of his own effort. In a collective sense we can see the effects of Cainism operating within our own American system. The most glaring example today is in the realm of American foreign policy on the Middle East. Cainism, couched in humanitarianism, imposes itself on the land of Israel insisting on a doctrine and policy for a Palestinian state coexistent with Israel.

Since 1948, the official United States foreign policy concerning Israel has been in accord with the United Nations resolutions for two states: a Jewish state, Israel; and a Palestinian state, Palestine. Did they forget God? It was He that officially declared that the land was forever given to Abraham and his descendants through his son Isaac. This was His sovereign choice, the Abrahamic covenant. (Ishmael had no inheritance in the land.) Nonetheless men have tampered with God's sovereign election of Israel and the specified land boundaries. Man's altruistic humanitarian justice ethic is the same as Cain's. It seems very just and righteous, but it is contrary to God's sovereign plan and choice. Today, not only is this the prevailing American position, but it is unfortunately shared by the United Nations. Notice the pervasive nature of Cainism.

These political machinations demonstrate human ideas that emanate from a kind of pathology that is sourced in a failure to grasp Cainism. Nonetheless, the collective wisdom of the state is not of God. It is collective corporate wisdom of Cainism coming to the forefront in our time, and it will certainly usher in the false peace of which Christ warned—and which the world is buying into wholeheartedly.

The effects of Cainism can also be seen in contemporary religion with its focus on self-esteem. In true Christian faith, Scripture instructs man to deny himself, take up his cross, and focus on loving God and loving his neighbor—as opposed to the modern philosophies of self-discovery. Yet, the pervasive power and self-righteous appeal of Cainism is causing great religious deception, even in the Christian Church. Many are unwittingly being set up for Cainism's crowning achievement: the Antichrist.

Some would argue that this is a harsh and unpatriotic attitude. Not if the cultural religious ethic is more exalted than the biblical ethic. The religious ethic as seen in our Pledge of Allegiance ("One nation under God") is nothing but a cliché with little or no spiritual reality. We are self-deceived into thinking we have a biblical worldview when, in actuality, we have a tainted American worldview laced with Cainism. This corporate self-deception is synthesizing in global dimensions and will finally congeal when the nations eventually establish a New Global World Order and a temporary peace. It will be the final, global rerun of Cain's offering.

No matter how grand the effort—even of the magnitude of a New World Order—mankind is still left with a stained conscience. We can't escape. This isn't to say that doing good is wrong, but we must accept the fact that doing good just isn't good enough to gain approval and acceptance with God. We are still left short.

When the spirit of nationalism (the synthesis of the spirit and will of the members of the nation state) rises higher than the Spirit that exalts Christ, the state has become deified—and its people have fallen into idolatry.

Cain was egocentric in that he thought he could better himself—and his position with God—on the basis of his own effort. He failed to recognize his inherent evil nature and God's solution for his predicament. In his confusion, Cain sought, through human endeavor and achievement, to establish his own righteousness.

Abel's sacrifice, on the other hand, was not aimed to impress God; rather, it was an astute recognition of his hopeless predicament. He cast himself on God, believing God was merciful. Thus, Abel's offering foreshadows Messiah's death on the cross as man's only means of salvation and recovery from his precarious condition (Hebrews 11:4). Herein lie the two principles that dichotomize the undercurrents of all human thought and behavior throughout human history: Since man cannot live with his guilty conscience, he either inadvertently selects Cain's approach to God or, if he is called, Abel's approach.

On the surface, Cainism appears more powerful, has more appeal, and seems more righteous. This is because it caters to the ego of man, and it gives expression to man's need for purpose and meaning in this life. This type of fulfillment is a temporal avenue and does not take into account God's eternal plan for mankind. Neither does it answer the need for an *eternal* answer and meaning for existence.

The collective guilt of the nations, arising as a result of ignoring Abel's sacrifice, provides an open door for the emulation of Satan's lust for power, as well as a reenactment of his pursuit of it. This is the driving force of the enormous effort toward the construction of a New Global World Order.

Abel's sacrifice, by prefiguring the cross of Christ, laid down the basis for restoration with God, a clear conscience, and, therefore, the ability to partake again of the tree of life—the life of God, which is love, joy, and peace.

All of history has been shaped by the two principles embodied in the lives of these two brothers. Cainism, with its refusal to concede to the inherent broken nature of man, strives vigorously, but futilely, for a self-adjusted righteousness through good works. Abelism represents the basis of the New Covenant, which rests on the foundation that "without shedding of blood is no remission [forgiveness of sin]" (Hebrews 9:22).

The worldviews of the brothers are in direct collision, and their concepts of self are directly opposed. They are totally irreconcilable and can never merge. The divergent philosophies that have been built on these two spiritual roots have affected the nature and expression of every human soul and nation state that has ever existed.

CHAPTER THREE

The Mark of Cain

> And the LORD set a mark upon Cain, lest any finding
> him should kill him.
>
> *Genesis 4:15*

The mark of Cain has been a point of discussion and debate since time began. Because Cain's descendants perished in the great Noahic flood, what the actual mark of Cain was has been left to speculation. There is no longer a literal mark. What has remained is the symbolic significance of Cain's mark and its new emergence in the mark of the Beast.

God marked Cain because he murdered his brother Abel. Actually, the mark represented Cain's allowing sin to have mastery over him. Cain could not master sin because he thought his good hard work would balance out any wrongdoings and, thus, make him a righteous man. He never came to recognize that sin was intrinsic to his nature. Cain was jealous and hateful toward his brother; it was his nature. As a result, Cain slew Abel. These two men, both literally and symbolically, represent the two principles that operate the human conscience and impact life throughout time, as we have already noted.

Abel's relationship with God is evidenced throughout history in the ancient sacrificial system of the Jews and, today, in the New Testament era through the sacraments of communion. But the greatest evidence is seen when a human life is transformed by the power of God. In the future, we will see it environmentally in the millennial reign of Christ.

Cain's system can be seen in the Gentile world governmental systems and in all religion where law is exalted. It's final form will be the Global World Government of the Antichrist, which is called the Beast system. The Beast and all whose names are not written in the Book of Life will be marked with the neo-mark of Cain, called the "mark of the Beast."

NEO-CAINISM

The mark of the Beast, mentioned in Revelation 13, is the representation of the world's greatest technological economic system and religious worship incorporated into an identification mark. The mark represents the highest corporate achievement of the human race, and it is the crowning work of mankind—the utopia of which men have dreamed since time began, man's futile attempt to return to a Garden of Eden.

The mark identifies all who receive it as those who believe in man, the finest, most altruistic qualities of the human being. It is a system that exalts man and defines him as the triumph of evolution. In other words, it encompasses everything that man is and all he has done collectively, from the beginning until now, and his final effort to establish world peace and safety in fortress earth.

This colossal effort is the last days offering of Cain once again. And once again it will be rejected by God. But all those who buy into the system—knowingly or ignorantly—will receive on their hand or forehead the neo-mark of Cain, the mark of the Beast.

What Is the Mark of the Beast?

In the pre-Christian era, there was one who was given great insights into these mysteries. His name was Daniel. He was one of the four great prophets of Israel. Daniel's prophetic writing reveals insights into the mysterious mark of the Beast.

God defined the nature of Gentile world empires as animalistic. Daniel portrays them in his visions as wild beasts without God as their ruling and controlling authority (Daniel 7:1-12). For example, Daniel saw the Babylonians as a roaring lion. The Medo-Persian Empire he characterized as a bear. The Greeks he saw as a leopard with two wings. The last ruling empire was different than all the rest. The last empire he explained as a beast which had no earthly counterpart; it had ten horns and one more little horn.

The apostle John, in the first century of the modern era (some six hundred years later), also caught a vision of this last beast. His description is found in Revelation 13. Here we find a strikingly similar representation of the last great world Gentile power that Daniel described in his writings. Curiously, we also find that this last great world Gentile power (the completed system) was actually brought to completion by another Beast, a second Beast that is described as one that had two horns and looked like a lamb but spoke like a dragon (Revelation 13:11). What was this second beast?

The Second Beast

This second Beast has been wondered and talked about for centuries. It is a confounding perplexity and a great and deep mystery. In addition to its identity, it uses principally three different abilities (powers/signs) or tools in finalizing the construction of the great Beast system (Revelation 13:13-18):

1. Fire that comes down from heaven;
2. An image that speaks and has spirit life'
3. A mark, which is 666, without which no one will be able to buy or sell.

The last of these three abilities is called the "mark of the Beast."

The mark of the Beast is the most talked about feature of the abilities of this two-horned Beast. The mark obviously relates to some kind of economic system that will do away with the necessity for gold, currency, or money as we have know it. It will be an economic system unlike anything that has appeared anywhere in history. It will be a system in which all the world will participate—or else go without buying or selling. It will be a system without currency. (See Chapter 29 for details.)

CHAPTER FOUR

Rebellion in Heaven

According to several Old Testament passages (see Ezekiel 28, Isaiah 14, and Genesis 1), prior to the creation of man, God set up His government in the spiritual realm with governing principalities. Three of the most powerful of these entities were archangels. Their names were Michael, Gabriel, and Lucifer.

Many today, especially in the western hemisphere and the industrialized nations, regard this history as mere myth. Very little credence is given to the existence of a spiritual realm. In these nations, utilitarianism and materialism tend to pervade the consciousness of the populace. The citizens of Western nations see very little need—nor do they place great significance on—the reality or existence of a spiritual world.

Nevertheless, Scripture records that God created spiritual beings to govern His kingdom. The most powerful and talented of all was Lucifer. The prophet Ezekiel was given great understanding into Lucifer's beauty, authority, and power (see Ezekiel 28:13-19).

Lucifer was God's chief assistant. He also had his own vast network of subordinates that assisted him in the work of governing. We would do well to consider this powerful position Lucifer had in God's government.

He was the angel who covered; that is, he was established to guard. His great beauty and splendor were unparalleled, his musical talent unmatched in all the universe. He was the master of commerce and trade.

Although God in His foreknowledge recognized what troubles the future held, He entrusted Lucifer with great knowledge, insight, wisdom, and understanding into the workings of His kingdom.

Lucifer's pride was insatiable. When he sought to usurp God's very throne, God's rule, he was cast from his position and imprisoned on a speck of dust called earth. What a judgment! His freedom and authority had spanned the infinite heavens, and now he was a convict imprisoned on a tiny planet somewhere in space.

God's anger would not rest with this expulsion alone. Lucifer's disloyalty created a tremendous void in heaven's government. Scripture records that a third of all the created beings in God's government were also cast out. Lucifer was able to carry off in his rebellion one third of the angelic host (Revelation 12:4).

The enormity of this loss, in earthly terms, would be like running the federal government with out the Congress; it would be a literal impossibility.

The Lord, in His foreknowledge, wasn't taken by surprise. He had a predetermined plan of recovery and restoration. He created man to take Lucifer's lost position. This added to Lucifer's judgment; he would be forced to witness his replacement being prepared right before his eyes.

When man was created he was assailed by this enemy Lucifer, known on earth as Satan. Mankind was deceived and enticed into following him. Since the beginning of human history, Satan has been working to gain total control over the earth by setting up his own government. Through deception he has used human instrumentation as a means to bring about this control, a government wherein he would rule and ultimately be worshiped. He demonstrated this same wickedness when he originally sought to possess God's throne, and now he has been implementing it on earth.

God, in His majesty and foreknowledge, intervened and interrupted Satan's attempt to destroy mankind: God sent His Son, Jesus, to rescue the human race. Nonetheless, Satan's government, as it currently gains momentum, will lead some to assume that Christ's rescue mission failed. There are even religious cults that claim this to be so, but it is far from the truth.

In the face of Satan's New Global World Order, the Messiah is calling for an elected people to follow him. These elect people, whom He calls His sons, are called from all nations and are in the process of transformation. Their character is being fashioned after the likeness of their Savior, Jesus Christ. This is God's purpose and process as they live out their lives awaiting the appearance of their true King. The contrast and conflict between these two warring governments is the cosmic venue of that process of transformation.

Furthermore, the saints must experience the effects of that conflict in order to fulfill their eternal destiny with Christ. They will face conflict and resistance from the forces allied with Satan's movement toward a Global World Order. This is to be expected.

The saints are required to resist the devil and to stand for righteousness. They are instructed to pray, "Thy kingdom come. Thy will be done in earth, as it is in heaven" (Matthew 6:10). They are required to "fight the good fight" (1 Timothy 6:12) and to "love not the world" (1 John 2:15).

This objective perspective is vital. The subjective human predicament and the pressure from environmental factors become so overwhelming that, without this objective point of view, it becomes exceedingly difficult to stand strong in faith.

We must have the insight to know what the enemy is doing. We must understand his plan so we are able to resist his deception and maintain the vigilance of faith.

What lies ahead is Satan's program for the New World Order.

CHAPTER FIVE

The Unseen World

Throughout Scripture, there are passages alluding to the spiritual realm which was formed by God before the material realm was created. Two of the most notable passages on this subject are in Isaiah 14 and Ezekiel 28.

> How art thou fallen from heaven, O Lucifer, son of the morning! how art thou cut down to the ground, which didst *weaken the nations!* For thou hast said in thine heart, I will ascend into heaven, I will exalt my throne above the stars of God: I will sit also upon the mount of the congregation, in the sides of the north: I will ascend above the heights of the clouds; I will be like the most High.
>
> *Isaiah 14:12-14 (emphasis added)*

Moreover the word of the LORD came unto me, saying,
Son of man, take up a lamentation upon the king of
Tyrus, and say unto him, Thus saith the Lord GOD;
Thou sealest up the sum, full of wisdom, and perfect in
beauty. Thou hast been in Eden the garden of God;
every precious stone was thy covering, the sardius,
topaz, and the diamond, the beryl, the onyx, and the
jasper, the sapphire, the emerald, and the carbuncle,
and gold: the workmanship of thy tabrets and of thy
pipes was prepared in thee in the day that thou wast
created. Thou art the anointed cherub that covereth;
and I have set thee so: thou wast upon the holy mountain of God; thou hast walked up and down in the
midst of the stones of fire. Thou was perfect in thy
ways from the day that thou wast created, till iniquity
was found in thee. *By the multitude of thy merchandise*
they have filled the midst of thee with violence, and thou
hast sinned: therefore I will cast thee as profane out of
the mountain of God: and I will destroy thee, O covering cherub, from the midst of the stones of fire. Thine
heart was lifted up because of thy beauty, thou hast
corrupted thy wisdom by reason of thy brightness: I
will cast thee to the ground, I will lay thee before kings,
that they may behold thee. Thou hast defiled thy sanc-
tuaries by the multitude of thine iniquities, by the iniquity of thy traffic; therefore will I bring forth a fire
from the midst of thee, it shall devour thee, and I will
bring thee to ashes upon the earth in the sight of all
them that beholdeth thee. All they that know thee
among the peoples shall be astonished at thee: thou
shalt be a terror, and never shalt thou be any more.
Ezekiel 28:11-19 (emphasis added)

Since the fall of Lucifer, there has been a powerful negative
force operating in this unseen spiritual realm. It has victimized
man in ways he simply cannot perceive. Satan has brilliantly
organized this world into a complex system of politics, economics, philosophy, education, culture, science, and religion.

RELIGIOUS DECEPTION

Although Satan operates in every area of deception, he is especially adept at religious confusion. As stated above, he was on the mountain of God. The term *mountain of God* refers in Scripture to the government of God.

> And the stone that smote the image became *a great mountain*, and filled the whole earth.
>
> *Daniel 2:35 (emphasis added)*

Lucifer's great understanding of the things of the Lord made it easy for him to arrange counterfeits of worship. The Eastern religions, for example, are masterpieces of religious confusion designed to deceive the multitudes. Space does not allow for a discussion of the world's vast array of religions—including some Christian groups—that have careened off the pathway of truth.

Since the discovery of the serpent in the garden, there has always been an evil executive power on earth for the completion of the goals of darkness. The end of it all will be a global kingdom for the devil himself. Through his ability to bring almost total obedience and worship to himself through a Global World Government, the world will see the results of his incredible, evil brilliance.

This multi-millennia process is speedily reaching its final form. When the millennial bug problem of the year 2000 threatened to shut down the world's computers, a massive, two-hundred-billion-dollar repair program further galvanized the global computer system. That event advanced the world toward the ultimate grip of darkness and its comprehensive control over the earth, thus paving the way to the mark of the Beast.

That there is a definite strategy at work to bring this about is stated and restated throughout the Old and New Testaments. The strategy is clearly evidenced throughout ancient history, and it was prominently and clearly displayed in the atrocities of Adolph Hitler's Third Reich in the past century.

UNFOLDING SATAN'S PLAN

It is not the intention here to speculate on the future but to lay out historic and current trends that are in alignment with the ancient prophetic writings. Therefore, what is being set forth is not intentionally predictive but, rather, interpretive, that we might clearly see the hour in which we live and how we should conduct ourselves.

> And let us consider one another to provoke unto love and to good works: Not forsaking the assembling of ourselves together, as the manner of some is; but exhorting one another: and so much the more, as ye *see the day* approaching.
>
> *Hebrews 10:24-25 (emphasis added)*

The day of Christ is rapidly approaching. We must stay attentive to the many signs of our times. Scripture predicts that there will be "wars and rumors of wars" (Matthew 24:6). Nation will rise up against nation. Famines, pestilence, and earthquakes are all part of the last days scenario that will overtake the inhabitants of earth. It is as though the earth is groaning, like a woman about to give birth. As we get closer to the end, these pangs will get more frequent and intense and be of greater duration. Scripture indicates that there will be *specific signs* to watch for, indicating the nearness of the day of the Lord. The most important of these signs is mentioned in 2 Thessalonians 2:13.

> Let no man deceive you by any means: for that day shall not come, except there come a falling away first, and that *man of sin [lawlessness]* be revealed, the son of perdition.
>
> *2 Thessalonians 2:3 (emphasis added)*

There have been those who tried to force this passage, by using the Greek text, to say the word *apostacia* actually means a departure from the earth. The word *departure*, they say, is actually a reference to the Rapture, the translation of the saints mentioned in 1 Thessalonians 4:16,17. But this is an unfortunate forcing of the scripture.

The rules of interpretation, hermeneutics, call for the weight of Scripture, meaning we must also look at what the rest of Scripture says about this topic. The weight of Scripture decidedly leans toward an interpretation of the word *apostacia* as a departure from *the faith*.

THE GREAT FALLING AWAY

> Now the Spirit speaketh expressly, that in the latter times some shall depart from the faith, giving heed to seducing spirits, and doctrines of devils.
>
> *1 Timothy 4:1*

Scripture points out that many would depart from the faith (see Matthew 24). This word *apostacia*, used in 2 Thessalonians 2, does not indicate a Rapture reference.

The context indicates that before the day of the Lord, there will be a time of *darkness* such as the world has never known. It is the powers of darkness that cause many people to abandon their faith in Christ. In the final onslaught, the powers of the evil one will cause many to be lost.

The loss of the restraining force (the Church) in the great falling away enables the Antichrist to appear and set up his world kingdom.

CHAPTER SIX

The Man of Sin

The Man of Sin will be manifest before the day of Christ.
The importance of this sign is noted by Scripture, and it is
the second clearest sign of the advancing day of the Lord.

> That ye be not soon shaken in mind, or be troubled,
> neither by spirit, nor by word, nor by letter as from us,
> as that the day of Christ is at hand. *Let no man deceive*
> *you by any means: for that day shall not come, except*
> *there come a falling away first, and that man of sin [law-*
> *lessness] be revealed, the son of perdition.*
> *2 Thessalonians 2:2-3 (emphasis added)*

The Church should be looking for the coming of Jesus by
paying attention to the advancing of the Antichrist and his system

called the Beast. The Antichrist will be the commander- in-chief of the notorious Beast system that was foretold in the books of Daniel and Revelation.

The signs of the day of the Lord were carefully pointed out to those who lived in Thessalonica. The Thessalonians were instructed to keep their eyes not only on the clouds but on the earth as well. Jesus said,

> And when these things begin to come to pass, then look up, and lift up your heads; for your redemption draweth nigh.
>
> *Luke 21:28*

WHERE TO LOOK

The prophet Daniel spoke of the people of the prince to come as the ones who would destroy the temple of God in Jerusalem (Daniel 9:26). The Romans, led by Titus, sacked Jerusalem in A.D. 70 and are those designated by Daniel as the people of the prince who is to come. Here we have a clue as to where the Antichrist will come from.

Today, the present day location of the old Roman empire is Europe, but there can be no doubt that *the scepter of the influence of Rome also shadows the United States*. He will be a Western man, and the location of his great kingdom will be in the area that comprised the old Roman Empire. That is because it was the Romans under Titus who, nearly two thousand years ago, began to set the stage for the coming world dictator. The Romans were the people of the prince to come to whom Daniel was referring.

The present day location of the old Roman Empire is Europe. Through the unification of the Common Market, by various treaties, economic ties, and the Euro, the stage is now set for the advent of the Antichrist. But we must be also mindful of the fact that it was the people of Europe that also founded the United States. *America also lies in the shadow and influence of Rome.*

How He Will Approach

By taking a look at the past we can see the unfolding of prophetic events. The spiritual cataclysmic event of Lucifer's mutiny and his resulting judgment—as presented in Isaiah 14, Ezekiel 28, and Revelation 12—bring out two key thoughts:

1. *Satan was cast down to weaken the nations.* The weakening of the nations, as Ezekiel pointed out, was affected by the abundance of trade, or merchandising.
2. *He has celestial beauty and spiritual knowledge.* He corrupted these traits and uses them to deceive the world.

Beauty, or appearances, and money, or mammon, are the instruments through which he brings confusion over all the earth.

Manifestations of His Agenda

The spiritual effect of Satan's control of the world can be most easily seen in the multitude of religions worldwide. But his agenda also includes a One World Global Government, with a man of his choosing at the head of it.

Satan has been working for thousands of years to set up his earthly throne. Now, two thousand years after the birth of Christ, we are very near the completion of Satan's world government. Let us trace the progression of his efforts.

CHAPTER SEVEN

The Mother of All Harlots

An understanding of Mystery Babylon's historical influence from Eden to present is imperative to understanding Satan's work in the world.

In the book of Revelation, perhaps the most infamous language that symbolizes the worldwide religious confusion is seen in the great harlot of chapter 18. We find her referred to in highly symbolic language: *Mystery Babylon, the Mother of Harlots.* Many have offered interpretations of this mystery woman, but by and large she is a false representation of God's true church on the earth. She goes about seducing the inhabitants of the earth through false doctrines and perverted ideas of God (Revelation 18:1).

In both Revelation 17 and 18 we see two facets of Mystery Babylon: Mystery Babylon, Mother of Harlots; and Mystery Babylon, the Great City. It is vital to make a distinction.

Mystery Babylon, Mother of Harlots, is clearly a global religious order that operates under Satan to deceive the whole world religiously. Mystery Babylon, the Great City, is a commercial industrial complex that operates in conjunction and coordination with this pseudoreligious matrix. This satanically infused mystical industrial complex is the foundation of the prophesied Beast system of both the prophet Daniel and the apostle John.

THE BIRTH OF THE BEAST

After the world was destroyed by the biblical flood, it was repopulated by Noah's sons, Shem, Ham, and Japheth, and their descendants. Nimrod, a descendant of Ham, began the organization of great cities, building the first great city, Babylon, in the post flood era (see Genesis 11:19).

> And Cush begat Nim'rod: he began to be a mighty one in the earth. He was a mighty hunter before the LORD: wherefore it is said, Even as Nim'rod the mighty hunter before the LORD.
>
> *Genesis 10:8-9*

The expression "he was a mighty hunter before the Lord" can carry a hostile meaning. The word *before* is sometimes used as meaning "against" the Lord. The Jewish encyclopedia says that Nimrod made all the people rebellious against the Lord.[1] During his time, Nimrod fit the picture of the Antichrist, who was predicted to come later. According to God's word to Eve, one day a deliverer would come. Scripture says:

> And I will put enmity between thee and the woman, and between thy seed and her seed; it shall bruise thy head, and thou shalt bruise his heel.
>
> *Genesis 3:15*

Many at that time believed Nimrod was the promised Messiah and looked to him as the savior of the world. There were many legitimate reasons why people felt this way.

He was a mighty hunter. Hordes of dangerous animals roamed the land, and people lived in constant dread. Nimrod hunted and killed the animals, trying to make life safer for the people.

He even conceived of greater ways to defend the people by building walled cities, the first of which was Babylon. It's not hard to see why he was venerated, admired, and revered by the peoples of the world and why they looked upon him as the promised one.[2]

Nimrod organized Babylon into a great, worldwide commercial center. Then he extended his influence into the surrounding areas, establishing his control and prominence. He later developed a religious system that was based on the arrangement of the stars (known as the zodiac), from which comes the idea of astrology. The word *babylon*, which in Hebrew means "the gate of God," also comes from a similar Hebrew root word *balal*, which means "confusion."[3]

Mystery Babylon, Mother of Harlots, and Mystery Babylon, the Great City, are both mentioned in the book of Revelation as the end time promulgators of Satan's program for world control. If the physical Babylon had remained, today it would be located in present-day Iraq. [4]

NIMROD, AN ANTICHRIST

It can be seen that Nimrod, the humanitarian heralded as a savior of the world, was a classical antichrist. He led the people away from worshiping the living God and into idolatry. He taught the worship of life through mystery religions and worship of the stars. He taught the worship of creation—and left the Creator out of the picture.[5]

The power of Nimrod's control over the known world can still be felt today. For example, the tradition of the Christmas tree during the season of the celebration of Jesus' birth is actually a stolen idea from the celebration of the birth of Nimrod. The Roman Catholic church adopted the idea, which was a world-renowned pagan tradition, and applied it to the birth of the Lord Jesus Christ.[6]

From the beginning, Satan's executive power has been behind the world political, economic, and religious empires, beginning with ancient Babylon. It will end with a Global World Government.

CHAPTER EIGHT

Tracking the Beast

The following Scripture expresses, in symbolic form, the panorama of Gentile world rule—from the Egyptian empire until the final Global World Empire is formed.

And the angel said unto me, Wherefore didst thou marvel? I will tell thee the mystery of the woman, and of the beast that carrieth her, which hath the seven heads and ten horns. The beast that thou sawest was, and is not; and shall ascend out of the bottomless pit, and go into perdition: and they that dwell on the earth shall wonder, whose names were not written in the book of life from the foundation of the world, when they behold the beast that was, and is not, and yet is. And here is the mind which hath wisdom. The seven heads are seven mountains, on which the woman sitteth. And there are seven kings: *five are fallen,* and one is, and the other is not yet come; and when he cometh, he must continue a short space. And the beast that was, and is not, even he is the eighth, and is of the seven, and goeth into perdition. And the ten horns which thou sawest are ten kings, which have received no kingdom as yet; but receive power as kings one hour with the beast. These have one mind, and shall give their power and strength unto the beast.

Revelation 17:7-13 (emphasis added)

THE SEVEN HEADS

This scripture pictures a relationship between Mystery Babylon, who is called the Great Harlot, and the infamous beast upon which she is seated. Her seated position suggests that she is in control and being carried by the Beast. Although much biblical scholarship has been put forth concerning the heads of the Beast as being literal mountains or literal hills (i.e., that the seven hills of Rome are the mountains upon which the Harlot sits, the Great Harlot being Rome), Scripture goes on to point out that the seven mountains are seven kings. The angel says they are seven regal mountains, seven kings, seven great ruling powers.

A mountain, or prominent elevation on the surface of the earth, is one of the common scriptural images, or representations, of a kingdom, regal dominion, empire, or established authority. So King David, speaking of the vicissitudes which he experienced as the king of Israel says, "O Lord, by Thy favor Thou didst make my mountain to stand strong" (Psalm 30:7).

The Lord, in His threat against the throne and power of Babylon, said:

Behold, I am against thee, O destroying mountain, saith the Lord, which destroyest the whole earth: and I will stretch out mine hand upon thee, and roll thee down from the rocks, and will make thee a burnt mountain."

Jeremiah 51:25

And the stone that smote the image became a great
mountain, and filled the whole earth.

Daniel 2:35

The seven heads are best explained as seven kings. The symbolism of the mountains or heads merely represent seven successive kingdoms. It can be argued that, although heads may be kings or kingdoms, they should not be looked at in successive order. The fact that five of the heads had already fallen, one was then in existence, and one was still future answers that objection.

Since the issue of succession of kings is proved in the above scriptures, the identity of Mystery Babylon, Mother of Harlots *cannot be* papal Rome. The woman sits upon empires that had already fallen before Rome existed, and she continues to outlive the empires that come and go. She rides upon empires, kings, powers of the world; she inspires, leads, and controls them. She is above them all, so that they court her and are bewitched and governed by her. They are governed not with the reins of empire but with the lure of her fornication. Mystery Babylon is none other than Nimrod's Babylon that continues to hold sway through time, outliving each successive empire even to this day.

Her doom is at the end of time, when she will receive her judgment. She, therefore, fills up the whole interval of time from the foundation of Babylon, the city of Nimrod, until the end of the age.

THE TEN HORNS

The last great empire of the Gentile rulers (the eighth head coming out of the slain seventh head) will consist of a ten member confederacy, which is essentially Roman in flavor with a ruling Antichrist.

The ten members of the Beast are spoken of as horns. A horn in Scripture is interpreted as a king or a kingdom. Daniel said:

Then I would know the truth of the fourth beast...and
of the ten horns that were in his head.... And the ten
horns out of this kingdom are ten kings that shall
arise.

Daniel 7:19,20,24

These ten kings or kingdoms give their power and authority
to the Antichrist for one hour, or a short time.

The seven heads represented in the vision are seven world
Gentile powers, or imperial heads, that have existed throughout
history. These seven heads will be the subject of our focus over
the next several chapters. Remember that the goal of this process
of investigation will be the revelation of the identities of both
the first and second Beast of Revelation chapter thirteen. It is
imperative that we study both Beasts, for it is through the identification of the first Beast that the necessary clues emerge for
the identification of the second Beast.

SEVEN HEADS

Each head in the symbol represents an imperial empire.
These imperial heads, along with the ten horns (and the little
horn of Daniel 8), comprise the entire Beast system that was,
and is not, and is about to come. It can be seen from this scripture that the Beast will not be just a last days phenomenon but
that it has been Satan's executive agent existing in some form for
more than five thousand years.

The last phase of the Beast system will evolve to a climax
where ten kings or kingdoms will give their allegiance to a man
(the Antichrist) who will operate the Global World Empire. This
evolutionary process began with the foundation of Babylon, the
Mother of Harlots, and has proceeded through each successive
world empire to the present (Revelation 13:1).

The construction of the Beast system corresponds with the
words of Christ when he spoke of the times of the Gentiles.
"And Jerusalem shall be trodden down of the Gentiles, until
the *times of the Gentiles* be fulfilled" (Luke 21:24, emphasis
added). The "times of the Gentiles" simply means the period of

time where the empires of the world are controlled by the Gentiles.

Many believe the times of the Gentiles ended when the state of Israel was formed in 1948. Others believed it ended when Jerusalem was recaptured by the Jews in 1967. But the end of the Beast system will come with its destruction, when Christ returns to establish His theocratic kingdom on the earth for one thousand years.

> Thou sawest till that a stone was cut out without hands, which smote the image upon his feet that were of iron and clay, and brake them to pieces.... And the stone that smote the image became a great mountain, and filled the whole earth.
>
> *Daniel 2:34-35*

This scripture points to the coming kingdom of God, which strikes the existing governing powers and topples them. It is a kingdom cut out without hands, which signifies a kingdom that is not man made. It will come at the end of the world, and it alone will destroy the kingdoms (the Beast) of the Gentiles (see Daniel 2:44,45).

THE SPIRITUAL TEMPLATE

Cainism and Mystery Babylon are, and always have been, the principle guiding powers of each subsequent and succeeding imperial head from its rise to its fall. These guiding powers will come to their zenith in the Antichrist's Global World Order. Revelation 17:10-11 provides a historical template showing each imperial head from the time of its beginning until the present.

The Beast—The System

> And there are seven kings: five are fallen, and one is, and the other is not yet come; and when he cometh, he must continue a short space. And the beast that was, and is not, even he is *the eighth*, and is of the seven...
>
> *Revelation 17:10,11 (emphasis added)*

John saw the Beast as a system which had evolved over the course of history. Daniel, however, saw forward to the last stage of the Beast system, with the Antichrist and the ten horns at the very end of the age. When John spoke of the eighth head, he was speaking of a revived world imperial system that had recovered from a head wound, or, as the Scripture put it, the wound of a great sword.

> And I saw one of his heads as it were wounded to
> death; and his deadly wound was healed: and all the
> whole world wondered after the beast.
>
> *Revelation 13:3*

Today there are some who think that the apostle was talking about a man that had been healed from a wound to the head. They believe that this alleged human being would then turn into the Antichrist, a satanic resurrection as it were. But Scripture speaks of an imperial head being resurrected, *not a human being*.

Unlocking the Mystery

To get at the mystery of who and what the eighth head is, we must see who the seventh head is because it precedes the eighth head (the eighth head is of the seven). Getting to the root of this mystery takes some digging; we must reconstruct the whole system in its entirety.

> And there are seven kings: five are fallen, and one is…
>
> *Revelation 17:10*

We will begin here with the statement "one is." What does this mean? This was clearly the world empire that existed during the time Jesus walked the earth. It was also the time when the apostle John was writing the great book of Revelation. It was the Roman Empire.

Moving backward from the Roman Empire, signified by the head that "is," the sixth head, there had been five world empires that had fallen, which were of the same dominating class as Rome. A brief look at history tells us with unmistakable certainty who these five empires were.

THE FIVE THAT HAD FALLEN

In retreating sequence (going backward in time), the five fallen empires were:

1. Greece, 330-145 B.C.
2. Medo-Persia, 558-330 B.C.
3. Babylon, 625-538 B.C. (under Nebuchadnezzar)
4. Assyria, 800-606 B.C.
5. Egypt,[1] 2500-1000 B.C.

These are the five kings that had fallen. Rome was the sixth, the one in Revelation 17:10 that "is." The task ahead is to identify the empire that is called the seventh, from which comes the eighth. First we will briefly walk through the five fallen kings looking for clues to the identity of the last two empires, the seventh and the eighth.

CHAPTER NINE

Mystery Babylon

C ritical in understanding the five fallen kings is how the ancient Babylonian kingdom of Nimrod relates to the empires that would follow it. Babylon, the mysterious system, is represented in the book of Revelation as a scarlet woman, or a prostitute, and is titled Babylon the Great, the Mother of Harlots, and of the Abominations of the earth (Revelation 17:5).

In Egypt, according to Hislop, the worship of the patron god and goddess, Osiris and Isis, can be directly traced to Nimrod, founder of the great Babylon, and his wife Semiramus.[1]

Nimrod was a man of renown upon the earth. He advanced his kingdom from Babylon into Egypt, Assyria, and other parts of the world. His greatness as a mighty hunter and the protection he afforded the masses by fortifying the cities with walls caused great admiration by the peoples of the earth.

It was through fortification that the peoples enjoyed peace and safety from the ever-present threat of wild beasts. Nimrod became legendary amongst the peoples of the earth for these mighty exploits.[2]

Hislop records that in his hunting expeditions Nimrod employed the horse, along with leopards, to track down animals. His renown became universal, and Nimrod was deified by men and hailed as a savior in the eyes of the people. The ancient Babylonian coins that picture a centaur (half horse and half man) is the actual depiction and memorializing of Nimrod.[3]

Yet for all the good he did for the people in saving and protecting them from destruction, Nimrod turned their hearts from God and onto himself.[4]

DESECRATED TRINITY

In ancient times, the recognition of the Trinity was universal in all the nations of the world; however, in the pagan world it was overlaid with idolatry. Nevertheless, the corruption of the idea of the Trinity proved how deep-seated this idea was in the breast of men. Pagan religion was replete with symbols that attested to this idea of a triune God.[5]

It was during the Babylonian era, that an important change occurred in the pagan concept of the Trinity. The triune God was clearly articulated in the Christian era, but during Nimrod's time there consisted a blasphemous idea of the Father, Seed (or Son), and Holy Ghost. It came to be thought of as the eternal Father Spirit of God incarnate in a *human mother* and a divine son. As a result of this alteration in the original idea of the triune God, the first person of the Trinity. the Father, was now overlooked. Now, with the change, the Babylonians focused their worship on a goddess mother and a son.[6]

Since Nimrod had expanded the sphere of his influence and power into Egypt, these people also began to worship the mother and the son under the names of Isis and Osiris: Isis the mother, Osiris the son.[7]

As Nimrod's fame spread, the Babylonian godhead became a universal focus of worship. In India, the gods Isi and Iswara are the counterparts of the Egyptian Osiris and Isis, and they are worshiped even to this day. In Asia, the same holds true with Cybele and Deous as the facsimile of the Egyptian duo. In pagan Rome, it was Jupiter puer. In Greece, the godhead was Ceres, the great mother with the babe at her breast, or Irene, the goddess of peace with the boy Plutus in her arms. Even in remote places such as Tibet, China, and Japan, evidences were found of this same pagan worship of a misunderstood idea of the Trinity.[8]

Hislop makes tremendous application of this perversion of the Godhead and its effect on papal Rome, where Mary and Jesus have become the Christian counterparts of Egyptian Isis (the mother) and Osiris (the son).[9]

THE WIFE OF NIMROD

The depth of this mystery is great, with many turns in the road. To be able to arrive at some clarity of thought concerning the issue, we must go to the origin and centerpiece of the mystery: Nimrod and his wife Semiramus.

Semiramus, who had been known as the wife of Nimrod, evolved as time passed into a lofty position as mother of Nimrod as well. In Egypt, Isis was the mother and wife of Osiris, but these were merely Egyptian names attributed to the great fortress builder Nimrod and his wife/mother Semiramus. In Egypt, Osiris bore the title "husband of the mother."[10]

One last point needs to be hammered home before we press on to the next fallen king. In the ancient book of the prophet Daniel, we read of a god called Alamahozine, the *god of fortification* (Daniel 11:38). Since Antichrist honors a god of fortification, it is important to identify what and who this god was.

> But in his estate shall he honour the God of forces: and a god whom his fathers knew not shall he honour with gold, and silver, and with precious stones, and pleasant things.
>
> *Daniel 11:38*

Although nowhere in antiquity can a god of fortification be found, there is great evidence of a *goddess* of fortification. Her name is Cybel, and she is always seen with her crown turreted, like the fortifications of towers. The reason for the towers of her crown was due to the fact that she erected towers in the cities she ruled over.[11]

Babylon was the first city erected after the ancient world was destroyed by the great flood. Ovid, the great historian, tells us that it was Nimrod's wife Semiramus, the first queen of that city, who was believed to have surrounded the city with brick. Semiramus, the deified queen, was the derivation of the worship of the goddess of fortifications. Cybel, with her turreted crown, was also known as Rhea; Semiramus was know as Rhea at times as well. Cybel was actually another name for Semiramus.[12]

But Semiramus (Rhea) did not build the walls alone. It has been kept as a matter of record by the Bible (and also through the ancient historian Megasthenes) that it was Nimrod who surrounded the Babylonian city with the wall. Yet, Semiramus gained the glory because, in the esteem of the ancient idolaters, she held a higher position than Nimrod after his death. All the characteristics and successes belonging to her husband were attributed to her. She was, however, the counterpart of the deity (that is, Nimrod deified) presiding over the bulwarks or fortress. From this we can see that the god of fortresses is none other than Nimrod. His deified name in Babylon was Ninus (meaning, "the son").[13]

EGYPT, FREEMASONRY, AND THE NEW WORLD ORDER

It is an admitted fact that the secret system of Freemasonry was originally founded on the mystery religion of the Egyptian Isis, the goddess mother/wife of Osiris. In Isis—the Egyptian counterpart for Semiramus, Nimrod's deified wife/mother—we have a very important connection with Mystery Babylon of the Masonic lodges of the church era in the Western world, both Europe and the United States of America.

What could have united the Masonic body and its mysteries—if the mysteries had not had particular reference to architecture and building and had the god of the mysteries not been celebrated for perfecting the arts of fortification and building?

These mysteries of Freemasonry, learned from Egyptian mythology and indirectly from Babylon, would be applied to fortress earth—the obvious relationship of Freemasonry to empire building and global planning for a New Global World Order.

CHAPTER TEN

Five Fallen Kings

THE FIRST FALLEN KING: EGYPT

The Egyptian civilization arose after Nimrod's ancient Babylon, and it is believed to be more than forty-five hundred years old. The Egyptian people were a very spiritual people and firmly believed in an afterlife. They held to the Babylonian notion of a pantheon of gods, and their spiritual history is well-documented. The most important archeological discoveries of their religious history can be found in the Valley of the Kings in Luxor, Egypt. There, on the walls of the caves of the entombed pharaohs, are the hieroglyphic codes that have maintained the record.[1]

The character of the images kept on the walls of the caves suggests a very curious sense of how the Egyptians perceived the spiritual world. The deities pictured have animal heads and human bodies. Such a strange synthesis suggests an implied quality of the animal and made identification of the deity easy.

The temple of Karnak was the country's largest, and it was dedicated to the god Amon Re, the sun god. The most important gods, however, were Osiris and his wife, Isis. Osiris ruled over vegetation and the dead. Isis represented the devoted mother and wife. Their son was Horus, the god of the sky.[2]

When kings ruled ancient Egypt, the Egyptians believed that each of the pharaohs was Horus in human form. This legend greatly strengthened the authority of the kings. Strengthened by this myth, their authority had tremendous impact on every aspect of the people's daily life.[3]

Although the earliest beginning of Egyptian society dates back some five thousand years, it wasn't until 1554-1304 B.C. that Egypt became the world's strongest power. Much of the prominence and power of the nation was a result of the large and permanent army and their advanced military techniques, which they had learned from earlier periods. The Egyptians also developed a galley-powered navy with which they made many military conquests into Southeast Asia.[4]

This great world empire, the first of the five heads of the Beast mentioned in Revelation, reached its height around 1400 B.C. under King Thutmose III, when he brought Palestine and Syria under Egyptian control.

The infamous Ramses II, the oppressor of the Hebrews, reigned during Egypt's five hundred years of world dominance known as Dynasty XIX. It was during his reign, however, that the great Egyptian empire began to decline.[5]

THE SECOND FALLEN KING: ASSYRIA

Clearly the influence of Nimrod was established in Assyria, as Scripture points out in the book of Genesis. The principle city of Assyria even bears the name of Nimrod (Ninus, his name deified, is the principle root of the city's name, Nineveh).[6]

The Assyrian king was known as the great king, the legitimate king, the king of the whole world. In the Assyrian kingdom the figure of a bull represented the king; the same word that signified bull also signified a ruler or a prince. The horned bull signified the *mighty prince,* which was a direct throwback to Nimrod, and represented all the great Assyrian kings.[7]

Although the Assyrian civilization can be traced back to 2000 B.C., its empire building actually took place around 800-606 B.C. The story of Assyria is mainly a story of the Assyrian kings. Some of the greater kings were Shalmaneser, Tiglath-pileser, and Esarharden. These kings, along with others, led a proud, cruel, and warlike race.

In many respects they were much like Rome. Just as Rome welded all the peoples of the Mediterranean world into a great empire, then scattered seeds of her civilization throughout the world, so did Assyria weld into a great empire the numerous petty, warring states and tribes of Western Asia. Afterward, she spread her civilization throughout her extended domains, which to a great degree she had received from conquered Babylon.[8]

As the empires that succeeded her evolved and came to the forefront, it is not an exaggeration to say that the great civilization of Greece owes much of her architecture, sculpture, science, philosophy, and mathematical knowledge to the Assyrian Empire.

Assyria was a mighty power for hundreds of years, but after the mid-600s (B.C.), she declined as a world empire. Babylon was again coming to the forefront as a world power.[9]

The mighty influence of the Nimrodian Babylon (Mother of Harlots) can be clearly seen in the Assyrian Empire.

THE THIRD FALLEN KING: BABYLON

Babylon had two runs as a world empire: Nimrod's Babylon, which was recorded in Genesis chapter 10, and dates back to 3000 B.C.; and Babylon, which arose to supplant the Great Assyrian Empire during the 600s, reaching its peak from about 625-538 B.C.[10]

The question might be asked, why was Nimrod's Babylon of old not considered as the first of the five fallen kings mentioned in Revelation 18?

A good, but improper, answer would be that if you started with Nimrod's Babylon you then would proceed forward to Egypt, then Assyria, Babylon again, Medo-Persia, and Greece. This would equal six fallen kings and would be too many to fit into the prophecy.

It could then be argued, however, that beginning with Egypt and finishing with Greece is forcing the Scripture to say what you want it to say. Nimrod's Babylon should be the beginning point!

This point of view is not an unfair argument, but when the whole of Revelation 17 is looked at, it becomes clear why this is not so.

> And there came one of the seven angels which had the seven vials, and talked with me, saying unto me, Come hither; I will shew unto thee the judgment of the great whore that sitteth upon many waters: With whom the kings of the earth have been made drunk with the wine of her fornication. So he carried me away in the spirit into the wilderness: and I saw a woman sit upon a scarlet coloured beast, full of names of blasphemy, having seven heads and ten horns. And the woman was arrayed in purple and scarlet colour, and decked with gold and precious stones and pearls, having a golden cup in her hand full of abominations and filthiness of her fornication: And upon her forehead was a name written, MYSTERY, BABYLON THE GREAT, THE MOTHER OF HARLOTS AND ABOMINATIONS OF THE EARTH.
>
> *Revelation 17:1-5*

From this Scripture it can be seen that Nimrod's Babylon is the fountain head, or the progenitor, of all the world's empires and sits atop them as a ruling power. It is the ruling posture of the woman (Nimrod's Babylon) that elevates her importance above the succeeding fallen kings (beginning with Egypt and ending with Greece) thus eliminating her as one of the fallen kings. As we continue on, each successive king emanates from her (Nimrod's Babylon) and continues to have intercourse with her.

Modern Babylon, or the second emergence of Babylon around 600 B.C., in her magnificence, is still talked about, with her hanging gardens that many consider one of the great wonders of the world. The great walled city built by Nebuchadnezzar, who later attacked Judah and carried the Jews off, was considered impregnable. The city was so tightly secured that the people had absolutely no fear of ever being attacked or overtaken.[11]

The Prophet Daniel in Babylon

The prophet Daniel prophesied during the time of the Babylonian captivity of the Jews, when the Babylonians had carried them off to Babylon. God had given him a revelation of the world empires that would succeed from the time of the Babylonian era all the way until the end of time.

During a dream he saw the world empires represented in a giant figure. The body parts of the statue represented each successive kingdom that would arise. The head of the figure, which was made of gold, represented Babylon; the shoulders and chest, made of silver, represented Medo-Persia; the hips, made of Bronze, represented Greece; and the legs, made of iron, represented Rome. The feet were made of iron and clay, which relate to the last stages of the Roman Empire (Daniel 2:31-42).

Daniel saw these world empires again in a later vision. In the later vision, the empires were depicted to him as animals or beasts (Daniel 7:3-7).

The Beasts

Daniel saw Babylon as a lion, Medo-Persia as a bear, Greece as a leopard, and Rome—different from all the rest—as a beast that had ten horns. These ten horns corresponded to the ten toes of the feet in the first vision of world empires represented by the statue (Daniel 7:4-7).

When the Jews were carried off to Babylon, strange things began to happen to their customs and traditions. Prior to their captivity, the Jews had been given the Law of God in the Ten

Commandments and various other statutes at Mount Sinai. These regulations were God's plan for how Israel was to be governed. God's regulations covered every aspect of their life, including holidays, customs, and behaviors that were in accordance with the Mosaic Law (as passed down in the book of Leviticus). Whether it was the temple purification rites, the concept of the blood atonement wrought through animal sacrifices, the civic responsibility of the citizens, or even the cultural aspects of their society, the *Law* ruled over all and was the absolute guide of the people. The *Law* was absolute referee, whether for one's conscience or for the state.

The Hebrew nation was truly a peculiar nation, a chosen people different from all the rest. They were set apart from all the Gentile nations, who fashioned their civilizations out of the Nimrodian Babylonian culture.

The Gentile's governing ideologies came from abstract notions about their deities, myths, and lore, which originated from Nimrod's Babylon, the Mother of Harlots. In this remarkable way, the world's empires—each arising and succeeding the other until today—have committed acts of immorality and have become drunk with pagan tradition and worship.

The Babylonians had their gods and goddesses Bel or Bal and Astarte and Ishtar, the goddess from whom comes the present Easter celebration. This is just a small indication as to how Babylon affects the world today. But the evidence as to how Babylon has impacted the world throughout time is enormous.

The Law of Moses Diluted

It was during the Babylonian captivity of the Jews that much of the orthodoxy of the Mosaic Law and its keeping began to be undermined and diluted by the culture of the pagan Babylonian Empire and its pervasive influence.

In Babylon, the Jews began to elevate the oral tradition above the written Law. Now, having been exiled to a far off land and without the centerpiece of the faith (the temple), the Jews had no purification rites available through animal sacrifices. The blood sacrificial system was ripped away from them. As a result, the corporate conscience of Israel began to compromise the Law. Special addenda to the literal interpretation of the Law were added, compromising the truth in a vain attempt to absolve the national conscience.

The oral tradition evolved and then was formalized with the Talmud, which is the written version of the oral tradition. As the national conscience retreated and darkened, the selected people of God began to entertain Babylonian Mysticism and the occult.

Babylon, the Root of Jewish Mysticism

The influence of Babylonian Mysticism on the Jews has endured through the centuries. Even in this present day, Jews consult and religiously study the Kaballah, which is the Jewish book of the occult taken from their time of captivity in Babylon.

The derivation of the Kaballah was the ancient Nimrodian system, which had been handed down to Babylon during the time of Nebuchadnezzar. In Babylon (the third fallen king), the Jews learned to sin the sin of the pagan nations: fornication with the Mother of Harlots.

THE FOURTH FALLEN KING: MEDO-PERSIA

In the later part of the sixth century B.C., the ancient history of the near and middle east culminated in the establishment of the Persian Empire (558-330 B.C.) by Cyrus and Darius the Great.

In remote times, some Aryan tribes separated themselves from other members of their families and sought new places to dwell on the plateau of Iran. The tribes who settled to the south became known as the Persians, while those who settled in the northwest mountain region became known as the Medes. The names of the two peoples were always closely associated.[12]

The Persians were destined to become the dominant tribe. Eventually, the Persian kings ruled over Egypt, Palestine, Syria, Asia Minor, Mesopotamia, Iran, and, for a time, Northwestern India and Trace. The empire stretched from the Mediterranean to Central Asia, and from the Black and Caspian Sea to the Persian Gulf and Indian Ocean.[13]

Under Cyrus the Great (whom Isaiah called "the servant of the Lord" some fifty years before Cyrus was even born; see Isaiah 45:1), the Medes and the Persians built a vast empire which lasted more than two hundred years.[14]

The empire—which was centered in Persia and called the Achaemeid Empire—included most of the known world. The Medes and the Persians came to power by the overthrow of the great Babylonian empire. God had told Daniel that this was going to happen because the Babylonians had gone too far in oppressing the Jews (Isaiah 43:14).

The impregnable city of Babylon was captured by diverting the Euphrates River. The Medes and Persians then entered underneath the great walls through the conduits where the river had watered the city.[15]

The fall of Babylon automatically carried with it a claim to the Babylonian possessions in the west. In both Syria and Palestine, the native peoples welcomed Cyrus as a liberator. He reciprocated by respecting local traditions and religious practices. The Jews of the exile were permitted to return to Jerusalem and to rebuild the temple.[16]

Persian Art Reveals Mystery Babylon

The Persians and Medes took their ideas of art from the Egyptians and the Babylonians, and they, too, worshiped gods and goddesses of nature, such as the sun, sky, and fire. They even believed that their gods had social powers, and so their lives, like those of the great empires before them, were highly controlled by myths.[17]

When Persia invaded Greece in the early 400s (B.C.), it was the beginning of the end. The Greeks were able to stop the expansion of that empire and to expel the invaders. Then came Alexander the Great, who in 331 B.C. conquered the Medo-Persian Empire. His empire extended from 323-145 B.C.

The Fifth Fallen King: Greece

During the time of Christ, Rome ruled the world, but Greece ruled the minds of men. Greece was the birthplace of Western

Civilization. Greece gave the world Plato and his most famous student, Aristotle. But, advanced as Greece had become in the study of law, medicine, philosophy, and public speaking, they, too, believed that a pantheon of deities watched over them.[18]

Dionysus, or Bacchus, the god worshiped in Greece, was expressly identified with Osiris of Egypt, who is, as we have mentioned, Nimrod (according to the great historian Orpheus).[19]

Bacchus is often seen in pictures holding an ivy branch in one hand and a cup in the other. The devotees of Bacchus carried the ivy branch bound around their necks, carried in their hands, or indelibly stamped on their bodies. This was because the Greek word for ivy was *kissos*, and Kissos was one of the names of Bacchus. Further, it must be noted that the name of Cush (who was the father of Nimrod) was properly pronounced "Kissioi" in Greek. It was through the name Cush that the priests became familiar with the ancient mysteries. Since Kissioi means Cush, then the branch of ivy that was of such prominence in all the Baccanalian ceremonies was an express symbol of Bacchus himself.[20]

Bacchus as the son of Cush, none other than Nimrod, took on the name of his father Kissos, the Greek for ivy. In fact, he was even called "The Real Branch." One of the names of the Messiah, as expressed in the book of Isaiah, was exactly that name: "The Branch." Attributing the name of the son of God to a pagan deity is utmost blasphemy. So the cup in the hand of the Great Harlot of Revelation, which is full of blasphemous names, can be seen in the Greek worship of Bacchus, or old Nimrod. The relationship of the Greek religion to the ancient Babylonian Nimrod comes through clearly.[21]

Can the multitude of names attributed to Nimrod—in symbolic form and from empire to empire—be anything other than the names that fill the cup of the Harlot who sits on top of the seven-headed and ten-horned beast of Revelation?

So he carried me away in the spirit into the wilderness:
and I saw a woman sit upon a scarlet coloured beast,
full of names of blasphemy, having seven heads and ten

> horns. And the woman was arrayed in purple and scarlet colour, and decked with gold and precious stones and pearls, having *a golden cup in her hand full of abominations and filthiness of her fornication.*
>
> *Revelation 17:3,4 (emphasis added)*

Nimrod's Babylon is the Mother of Harlots that has deceived the whole world, even to this day. Examples can be found in the Christianizing of pagan holidays such as Easter (originally the worship of Astarte) and Christmas (Birth of Nimrod, son of Cush).

Very briefly, the first five world empires that are mentioned in Revelation 17 as having fallen—which correspond to the first five heads of the Beast—have been put forth. Where they all came from has been explained, along with how they were shaped and influenced by their mother, Nimrod's Mystery Babylon, the Mother of Harlots.

To recap, here they are again (this time from oldest to youngest in their ascending order):

1. Egypt
2. Assyria
3. Babylon
4. Medo-Persia
5. Greece

> And there are seven kings: *five are fallen,* and one is...
>
> *Revelation 17:10 (emphasis added)*

The sixth kingdom upon which the Harlot sits is Rome.

CHAPTER ELEVEN

Rome: The Sixth Empire

The empire that was begun according to tradition by the twin brothers Romulus and Remus, two shepherd boys, grew from a small community of sheep herders to an enormous empire of more than seventy million people. The city was situated next to the Tiber River atop seven hills (actually there are eleven hills), and far enough inland that it was protected from marauding bands of pirates. These natural barriers protecting the city enabled Rome to grow over the centuries, becoming the sixth empire of the world.[1]

Its beginnings date back to 735 B.C., and by 275 B.C. it controlled most of the Italian peninsula. Rome peaked at about A.D. 100 and fell in A.D. 476. During its peak it extended as far north as the British Isles and as far east as Persia. Rome was the capital city of the Roman Empire, and it was inhabited by more than two million people at its height. The glue that held the empire together was the *Pax Romana*, the Roman peace.[2]

The peace was maintained by a huge army that continued to grow as immigrants trickled into the empire, many of whom were recruited into the military. The army had three hundred thousand men.

The Roman law was the rule enforced by the might and strength of the military, which brought this peace. Although Republican institutions of government were kept throughout the history of the empire, it was the emperors who held absolute rule. They nominated the consuls and appointed new senators. The citizens' assemblies had little power. Emperors also headed the army and directed the making of the law. The authority of the Roman emperor overruled any act of the Senate.[3]

After an emperor died, the Romans worshiped that emperor as a god, similar to the Egyptians' worship of the pharaoh. It was emperor worship that provided a common base of loyalty throughout the empire. The Romans adopted the worship of the Greeks. They believed that the gods controlled nature, but they changed the names of the Greek gods to Roman names. The emperors were the supreme voice of the land superstitiously submitting to the pagan gods.[4]

Although much great romantic literature has been written about Rome, the prophet Daniel saw it as a ferocious beast. He spoke of Rome in more violent terms than all the rest of the world empires that had come before it (Daniel 7:7).

It was a restless kingdom that was not content with its size, and it continually overwhelmed new areas of land and peoples. Perhaps the reason for its fall in A.D. 476 was due to its own weight.

The Roman Empire must be remembered for the fact that it relished the spectacle of organized murder in the gladiatorial games, where men actually died for the amusement and enjoyment of the emperor and the populace. It was also for great sport that Christians were fed to lions. But foremost, Rome must be remembered for being the sixth great empire of the world, and murderer of the King of kings. What an epitaph! It was the empire that the apostle John wrote of when he said, "five are fallen, and *one is*," (Revelation 7:10, emphasis added).

CHAPTER TWELVE

The Seventh Head

> And I stood upon the sand of the sea, and saw a beast
> rise up out of the sea, having seven heads and ten
> horns, and upon his horns ten crowns, and upon his
> heads the name of blasphemy.
>
> *Revelation 13:1*

Historical ignorance creates a kind of blindness that obstructs the ability to gaze into the future. If one cannot see where he has come from, he certainly will not see where he is going. When it comes to a knowledge of world history, Americans, including Christians, have very little understanding of the past.

But of greater significance and perplexity is the historical blight of knowledge within the great theologians and spiritual leaders of the North American church. Their willingness to be coaxed along in a red-blooded American nationalism seems to blind them to a truly objective understanding of who we Americans are and where we came from.

AMERICAN ROOTS

When it comes to an understanding of Great Britain, the mother country, Americans are totally in the dark. Americans have become ingrown and isolated from the world by our tremendous wealth and the great oceans that surround us like a moat. These factors have created a corporate aloofness that insulates our nation from the rest of the world. Most Americans simply do not care about historical facts relating to their own national identity.

As the world stampedes toward a New Global World System, Americans must not lose sight of their European roots lest they become disoriented and miss an objective understanding of who they are as a people.

Since America was founded and established by Europeans, namely refugees from Great Britain, there should be at least a modicum of knowledge concerning the mother country. The roots of the American spirit began with the corporate soul of the founding forefathers, who came from Great Britain. Hence, we should study the environment that shaped the men who laid the foundation for this great and powerful nation.

GREAT BRITAIN

The history of Great Britain tells how a small island off the mainland of Europe grew to become the world's most powerful empire. During the time of its existence, and in the context of all history, there had not been a world empire like the British Empire.[1]

It was the industrial revolution of the 1700s that made Britain the world's richest manufacturing country. After 1815, the city of London became the vatican of world banking.[2] The empire was so enormous that the sun never set on it. By 1799 the empire covered about a fourth of the world's land and about a fourth of its people.[3]

Since people generally do not like to speak in disparaging terms concerning their own heritage, it is a difficult chore to lay bare the truth of the British Empire without bringing some degree of offense. Nonetheless, there are vital, hidden facts about the British Empire, which make biblical prophecy ever more clear.

Consider the thoughts conjured in the mind of English-speaking people when they speak of the British Empire? What was the British Empire? What really was behind this allegedly Christian empire?

In searching world history from the time of the fall of the Roman Empire, no other *world* empire had arisen since then, except the British Empire. It is the only one. *Is it possible that the British Empire is represented by the seventh head of the Beast of Revelation chapter 13?*

The apostle John saw a vision while exiled on the Isle of Patmos in A.D. 90. In symbolic form, he saw a beast coming up out of the sea. It had seven heads and ten horns. Six of these heads have already been identified in the preceding chapters, and now, as history is searched since the fall of the sixth head Rome, *another world empire, the British Empire, has arisen.* "And there are seven kings; five are fallen, and one is, and *the other is not yet come*" (Revelation 17:10, emphasis added).

But for some strange reason, neither North American nor Northern European theologians have ever considered the emergence and existence of the British Empire as the fulfillment of the seventh head of the Beast. The fact is, the British Empire is the *only world empire that qualifies* since the fall of the Roman Empire and, therefore, the only possible fulfillment.

The amazing power of this vast, worldwide empire did not reach its zenith—and its true status as undisputed ruler of the earth—until Napoleon was defeated at the Battle of Waterloo in 1815. When the British finally conquered the French, the British Empire ruled the world for about one hundred years, from 1815 until the outbreak of WWI.[4]

THE GLOBAL RULE

In 1815, the British Empire, the seventh imperial head of John's Beast, emerged as supreme power over the area that essentially encompassed the old Roman Empire.

However, while the British Empire increased in power, it was specifically accruing to the revenues of *The City* under the crown, not to England itself. (The city of London fell under the control of an elite group of bankers, the Rothschilds. More explanation of this international elite will be given shortly.)[5]

The City today controls over 80 percent of all international business transactions. England itself was bled dry by this hidden inner government and was harnessed for the special aims of The City, which became the seat for an International Global World Government.[6]

The internationalists (the bankers) have no feeling of nationalism or patriotism towards any nation, including England. England—once Christian-controlled, to a degree, under the influence of the Protestant Reformation—fell under the power of "mammon" or money, controlled by the international money cabal (the Rothschilds).[7]

(*Note*—This is not to dismiss the important workings of the Holy Spirit in England during those times. God did profound things in the eighteenth and nineteenth centuries in England. The religious zealots who founded the United States were people who came from Britain and had a deep, orthodox knowledge of the Scriptures. But the secular English state tried to control the operation of the true church, and this became intolerable for true believers. This was one of the key motivating issues for the exodus to the New World.)

The East India Company

Little, if any, is known in the western hemisphere of the nefarious ways in which the British Empire gained its supremacy over the earth. However, the peoples of India and China can give grim testimony to the most notorious of all the terrible war machines of conquest that the Empire possessed: the infamous East India Company.[8]

The company was formed in 1600 when, following the defeat of the Spanish Armada, Queen Elizabeth granted a charter to certain London-based merchants to trade in the East. The company grew stronger as it became ensconced in worldwide trade. It was allowed to have monopolistic privileges in return for a fraction of its earnings, and so it gained tremendous financial might. As it grew, it built a large private army which contested with the French and Dutch traders and learned methods of control and looting in India. India became controlled by bribery and graft as the company set up a puppet government, which then imposed forced sales of merchandise and outright looting through tax collecting. If the people resisted, various methods of compulsion were practiced—such as fines, imprisonment, and floggings—forcing the people to submit.[9]

The British taxed the people to exhaustion, and when famine conditions arose in 1770 due to poor weather, ten million people in Bengal starved to death.[10]

East India House

Towards the end of the seventeenth century, when America's war for independence from the iron-like grip of British dominion was succeeding, the political circles associated with the British East India Company *seized nearly complete control over British political party affairs.* The historical significance of this event—and its subsequent effect on world affairs—has been monumental, and yet it is completely neglected in this hemisphere.[11]

A new prime minister came on the scene: William Petty. At that time Petty negotiated the peace treaty with the U.S.A. (after the war for independence); he also directed British intelligence services in a complex worldwide task of conquest and subversion. Even though the American Revolution had succeeded, in the eyes of this man it was not the end of the effort to subjugate the American colonies to British control.[12]

Over in India, a board of control for the affairs of India was set up under the leadership of Henry Dundus. Dundus controlled the Indian operation for thirty years, during which time he proposed that Indian opium be poured into China as an instrument of war and looting. Dundus was also the man to whom Aaron Burr, vice president to Jefferson, reported in England.

In 1787 Dundus wrote a master plan to extend the opium traffic into China, and he personally supervised the worldwide traffic of opium which had been escalated by the East India Company.[13]

After the war, General Cornwallis, the British general who surrendered at Yorktown, was reassigned by Dundus to be commander in chief and governor general over India. Britain was gearing up for a military offensive over all Asia. Finally, in 1803, the British East India Company subdued and controlled the entire subcontinent of Asia. The army had now swelled to more than a quarter million men, and the navy patrolled the seas from the southwest Pacific to the Persian Gulf. This power engaged in conflict after conflict, inflicting fatalities in the millions.[14] But people in the western hemisphere are routinely ignorant of such facts of history.

To further loot India, the British raised high tariffs but kept India open for British goods. India paid for its imported goods from Britain by opium from plantations developed by the British. The opium was sold to the Chinese to oppress them and to raise money to pay for the British goods sold to India.[15]

The peasantry, those who cultivated cotton, were treated with savage and revolting actions. They were subjected to torture and every effort—lawful or unlawful—to extract revenues. When they tried to run away from this brutal treatment, they were rounded up by the British, flogged, and put back to work. As the nation's cotton began to disappear due to this kind of treatment, the exploiters looked to American slave cotton as a viable alternative source of cheap raw material.[16]

The British occupation of India was maintained and manipulated by a cunningly devised cultural warfare. The idea for maintaining control was to prevent any and all importation of Western ideals or values into western India.[17] The East India Company patronized and advanced the most outrageous aspects of the pagan Indian religions and made Hinduism and Islam British state-run religions.

When the British finally turned their gaze upon America, the technique they used was to displace the Western, Christian beliefs of the American people by importing and introducing Eastern Indian religious beliefs, thus undermining Western values. The drug wars can also be traced to the East India House strategy.[18]

"To destroy a country," Solzhenitsyn wrote, "you must first cut its roots." If America's roots are in the Judeo-Christian values and traditions, they have, in large measure, been severed. Today, of course, the root base of the philosophy of the New Age movement is directly taken from Indian Hinduism.

JOHN STUART MILL

The chief intelligence officer of the East India Company into the 1900s was John Stuart Mill, who ran the evil organization from London. When the Indians revolted in 1857, the atrocities of that conflagration so outraged the world that Queen Victoria stepped in, and within a few years the East India Company was dissolved. But the industrious John Stuart Mill turned his attention to the fledgling nation of America. He was ready to apply the knowledge gained from his many years of experience in India to the conquest of America.[19]

Before we delve into the subversion of America by the East India Company, it must also be said that the East India House in London became the central point of interaction and dialogue for the main antagonists of Western Civilization. This central location became the seat of the existential writers that focused on a theology of man as the center of all things. The propagators of this "Anglicized Hinduism" were men like Henry David Thoreau and Ralph Waldo Emerson. Charles Darwin was also contemporary with these men, and he associated with them at the East India House. Their doctrine was the philosophical base from which worldwide cultural warfare would be launched.[20]

The advancement of the New Age movement can actually be traced directly to this think tank, which operated in London at the East India House run by John Stuart Mill, the oppressor of India.[21] These men did not believe in the creed of all men being created equal but, quite the contrary, that all men by nature were created unequal: that some were meant to rule and others to be ruled over. They saw the biblical definition of man submitting to a sovereign Lord God as repugnant to their dreams of globalism. Empire building, in their thinking, began with a definition of man as central, and from that point all considerations would proceed. The colonies in America, which were becoming more and more prosperous under the biblical theology of man, had to be finally conquered and brought under control.[22]

GOVERNMENT AND MAN'S NATURE

The American Constitution was built upon a foundation that had its roots in a biblical definition of man. The writers viewed man as having fallen from a divine position with God. They saw that man had become corrupted and that he has a sin nature. The founding fathers reasoned that because absolute justice and objectivity was possessed by God alone, no man, by himself alone, was fit to rule. They wrote the Constitution very cautiously. They placed checks and balances into the structure of the government so that one single man could never gain absolute control. They despised the monarchial system of Europe and England.

There were to be three branches of the federal government: executive, judicial, and legislative. Each branch was to insure that no one man or group of men could gain absolute political power; each branch would balance the others. Tantamount in their thinking was the elimination and cruelty of despotism. This was the very issue over which they left England.

The framers of the Constitution had a keen sense of British history when they sat down to write the Constitution. They clearly had in mind the historical facts of the evolution of the monarchial system in England.

THE MONARCHIAL SYSTEM

When Henry VIII became king of England in the sixteenth century, he was already wed to Catherine of Aragon. When he sought to divorce her and wed Anne Boleyn, it caused a separation between Henry and the Pope. The Roman Catholic Church refused to sanction the marriage. Nevertheless, King Henry went on with the marriage and was excommunicated from the Roman Catholic Church. Henry then ordered the English Parliament to declare the King as the supreme head of the Roman Catholic Church of England.

The separation of the Church of England from Rome effectively brought the Protestant Reformation to England. In 1534, by Henry's insistence, Parliament passed two acts that made the break complete. The first declared that the Pope had no authority in England. The second declared the Church of England a separate institution with the king as its head (the famous Supremacy Act). Both church and state had come under the authority of the king.

It was this act by King Henry VIII—bringing the religious and secular under one roof—that eventually led to the reasoning behind the first amendment of the United States Constitution. The spirit and intent of that amendment was not to eliminate religion from its influence on government but, quite the contrary, to keep government out of religion.

Later, both Henry's son and Queen Elizabeth caused the work of establishing the Church of England to go forward. Upon the arrival of the 1600s, England was ready to embark on a great era of development.

When the English, through the leadership of Sir Francis Drake, defeated the Spanish Armada in 1588, England had become the undisputed ruler of the seas. She now controlled all the shipping lanes, exacting tribute for maritime activities from all of Europe.

The last piece of contrivance for realization of a Global World Empire was the ability to subjugate nations of the world through the sheer power of capital and credit.

THE BATTLE OF WATERLOO

The opportunity for the seizure of "mammon" arose during Napoleon's attempt to seize Europe at the famous Battle of Waterloo. How was the Battle of Waterloo utilized to further the aims of those who sought for a New World Order?[23]

The French Revolution

First it must be understood that the real force of the French Revolution was not a spontaneous explosion within the corporate breast of the collective lower class of France. Historians have long blamed the masses for the revolution. However, enough facts have come to light to prove that France was infiltrated by subversives of the internationalists to destabilize her into a chaotic mass. Why was France selected as the beginning of the global revolution for a New World Order?[24] The internationalists based in England saw in France a formidable opponent to the aims of the centralization of European capital.[25] France had to be destabilized into chaos. Then, with the important defeat of Napoleon, the opportunity arose to seize financial power into the hands of the money conspirists. While the philosophical intrigue and planning to upset the unifying aspects of monarchical family intermarriage shifted temporarily to center on Bavaria and the German states,[26] the war chest of world revolution was being concentrated and built in London.[27]

The Rothschilds Seize Control

Here is how it occurred. Upon the Battle of Waterloo hung the future of the European continent. If Napoleon were successful, France would be the undisputed master of Europe. If Napoleon were defeated, England would reign supreme.[28]

Obviously, the success of Lord Wellington would have tremendous positive implications on the British stock exchange. With Nathan Rothschild positioned in London, the headquarters of the Rothschild banking dynasty, the stage was set for the soon-to-be financial rulers of the nations. As the armies closed in for the battle, the secret agents of the Rothschilds gathered the information to whisk back to London.[29]

When the outcome of the battle was known to Nathan Rothschild, he gave the signal for his people to begin quietly selling consuls on the stock market. As the consuls began to pour onto the market, it created a stampede that caused the market to fall and then cascade into a panic sell off. It was feared that Napoleon had won the battle and Rothschild was privy to this information.[30]

Unbeknownst to those outside his circle, Rothschild was manipulating the market downward so that he could buy up the consuls at five cents on the dollar. When the news hit that the

British had actually defeated Napoleon, the market soared like an eagle. Thus, Rothschild and his banking kingdom had seized, in one day, the vast war chest for the economic control of the nations.[31]

The Rothschilds were of Jewish descent, and England, being a Christian nation, was not inclined to allow Jews into positions of political decision making. Rothschild's response to this racist policy was this: "I care not for the laws of the nations. Give me the wealth of the nations and I'll make the laws."[32]

BANK OF ENGLAND

Now, with an understanding of the Rothschilds, we must backtrack through English history to the year 1694. This was the year the Bank of England, a privately owned bank called the Central Bank, was established. The establishing of the Bank of England was of no small importance in world history. It was utilized to advance the power of the City of London, hence, the entire affairs of the rapidly growing British Empire.[33]

When Rothschild pulled off his seizure of the British economic system, he also gained control of the Bank of England and the City of London. With the demise of France and the English victory over Napoleon at Waterloo, England in 1815 emerged as the undisputed ruling power of Europe. The power of "mammon" was now in their grasp, the monarchical headship was removed, the influence of the Church of England was minimized in state affairs, and all state matters were subjugated to the Barons of Finance.

CHAPTER THIRTEEN

The Innate Drive

> And I saw one of his heads as it were wounded to
> death; and his deadly wound was healed: and all the
> whole world wondered after the beast.
>
> *Revelation 13:3*

Profound events in Europe were taking place that were setting the stage for the death of the empire by a blow of war.

Behind the internationalists' drive toward a Global One World Government is a strange, innate sense of humanitarianism. It's as though the mandate to convert the world to a global village is their providential lot. It is the same driving force that Cain had when he offered to God a sacrifice of vegetables: man's human effort to right his twisted conscience. Globalism is the epitome of man's effort to bring about peace. The globalists seek to do this through the unification of the earth, but their misguided zeal is channeled through human contrivance and manipulation. The overriding mental gymnastic to bring this about is through the dialectic, *the ends justify the means,* or whatever it takes to get the job done. If it means trashing a human here or a nation there—whatever the cost—it is justifiable in light of the highly prized and desired goal. This is the rationale of those seeking global revolution and a New Global World Order.

The Internationalists' Apparatus

These internationalists seek the humanitarian goal of world "peace and safety." Their goal seems noble and virtuous, and, because of this, there are few who challenge their means. The means for pulling off this humanitarian extravaganza is quite a story. Ironically, the internationalists use the device of war as a means to peace.

The Money Machine

The internationalists will always profit from war because it doubly indentures a nation. First, it causes a nation to borrow in order to build its war machine; second, the nation has to borrow again after the war to rebuild its infrastructure.

Initially, the creation of nuclear weapons also served the interest of the money powers. Indebted nations that would dare to think of repudiation or a debt moratorium were brought back into tow by the threat of nuclear attack. Nuclear weapons were the ultimate collection agency tool. But this nuclear exclusivity is no longer the private province of the internationalists. The world is far more volatile now then in the fifties and sixties.

CHAPTER FOURTEEN

World Wars I and II

When America's industrial might was harnessed by the creation of the Federal Reserve System, the mobilization of credit became available to finance a New Global World Order. All that needed to be done was to create a world war. Most historians will admit that although there were two world wars, World War I and World War II, they were ostensibly one war with a period of cessation in between. They would also admit that the beginning of World War I had no apparent rationale behind it.

The Archduke of Austria was assassinated and, as a result, the whole world went to war. Why? To this day there seems to be no clear answer, unless one sees that the international bankers had everything to gain by a world war. After all, there would be great profit in making huge loans to so many countries.

The international debt that accumulated after these two wars staggers the imagination. What an incredible money machine! Remember:

The borrower is servant to the lender.

Proverbs 22:7

The gigantic cash flow from the interest of mega-loans to the nations would be used to create a New World Order after the pattern suggested by Engels and Karl Marx, whose principles were based upon Adam Weishaupt's Order of the Illuminati.[1]

WOODROW WILSON

During his second campaign to become president, Woodrow Wilson campaigned under the slogan, "He'll keep us out of the war." However, within only months of his inauguration he drew America into World War I. America began to borrow heavily both to build up its war machine and to finance a war on the other side of the earth. Many claim that Wilson was a pawn in the game of international power and world politics.[2]

The "war to end all wars," as it was called, served the internationalists in two ways: it brought the world into terrific debt and it prepared the nations to seek peace at any price. As the war dragged on, the nations became weary and were suffering from great debt. They were now prepared and ready to make sacrifices on the altar of peace and, to a great degree, their national sovereignty.

THE LEAGUE OF NATIONS

A League of Nations was proposed by Woodrow Wilson, which was the first step toward organizing the world into a One World Global Government. Wilson, who was manipulated by his mentor, Colonel Edward House, put forth the plan for the League of Nations in his famous fourteen points.[3]

Wilson's plan for a New World Order was well received by all nations except his own, the United States. Patriotic Americans saw the danger of such a setup and throttled the idea of the League. Wilson failed, and he died a broken man. So did the bankers' first attempt for a New World Order.

COUNCIL ON FOREIGN RELATIONS

The Council on Foreign Relations (CFR) was created by the globalists after World War I because of the League's failure. Its purpose was to monitor and determine American foreign policy so that America's decision making with regards to the nations of the world was in step with the ultimate goal of a World Government. The ground work for the CFR was laid by Colonel Mendel House, who was acting as the internationalist's agent in America.[4] More will be said in a later chapter on the CFR.

THE RUSSIAN REVOLUTION

During the final years of World War I, the Russian Revolution was carefully planned and tried. The Bolsheviks trained in New York, were financed by the international Kuen Loeb & Company (a New York banking house), and were sent through Germany into Russia to overthrow the Czar.[5]

The Bolsheviks were aided by Max Warburg, who was brother to Paul Warburg, the architect of the Federal Reserve System. Max was in control of the German banking system.[6]

But why bring about the perfect neo-feudal state in Russia first? The plotters had several reasons: It was the largest land mass between Europe and Asia, and the outbreak of globalism as a system could be more easily managed; its population was large enough to mobilize and easily conquerable; its technology was lagging and its financial power was easily assailable.

The setup for globalism in its final form would begin in Russia, but its conception and financing were formulated by the banking elite of Europe.[7]

ORCHESTRATION OF WORLD WAR II

As the bankers from Wall Street (J.P. Morgan & Co.) moved to rearm Germany, the aspiring Adolf Hitler viewed both the Bolshevik Revolution and the attempt for World Government through the League of Nations as a Jewish plot to take over the world. He saw the bankers as the principle movers and shakers in this gigantic effort.[8]

"The Protocols of the Learned Elders of Zion," of dubious origin, was cunningly leaked to Hitler by the world planners to deceive him, making him think the New World Order was a Jewish plot.[9]

Seventh Head Slain

World War II—which actually was a resumption of World War I—was, in the mind of the world planners, a necessary evil. The British Empire had to be dissolved.

The "great sword" that wounded the seventh head of the Beast was the one war (what we refer to as World Wars I and II) that brought the seventh head, *the British Empire*, to an end. After World War II, the British Empire ceased, but it should be carefully noted that the seat of global financial power remained in London, unscathed by war. In fact, the money powers became more powerful, due to the massive indebtedness the wars created.

In the Bible it is asked, "Who is able to make war with [the Beast]?" (Revelation 13:4). Yet the seventh empire was killed by the sword of war. What entity, what government, what other opponent out there could launch a conflict against the seventh head? When it can be seen how World War I and World War II were orchestrated by the international bankers—who had no allegiance to England or the British Empire, but merely used them for their purposes in accomplishing a Global World Empire—the question is answered. The seventh head was slain by a sword of its own creation.[10]

CHAPTER FIFTEEN

The Great Sword

ENTER HITLER

Hitler's Third Reich was supported and built by international capital, much of it coming from Wall Street, as the internationalists prepared the world for another blood bath and another round of debt.[1]

The need for the resumption of conflict was evident in that without the United States in the League of Nations, a World Government was impossible. What was needed was more debt and more cries for peace. Hence, the war needed to be rekindled.

When Hitler arose and began to foment such vehement hatred toward the Jews, it was because he believed he saw a Jewish conspiracy in a group of Jewish bankers who had seized control of the world banking system. He failed to see that the small group of bankers also included Gentile banking houses.[2] Germany's woes were not the fault of world Jewry.

Hitler blamed the whole of Jewry for the heavy-handed shackles of the Treaty of Versailles which ended WWI. He believed Germany was in ruins due to the Jews.

HITLER'S HATRED MANIPULATED

Then, adding fuel to the fire, Hitler's hatred was enflamed by the falsified document of "The Protocols of the Learned Elders of Zion."[3] This document was allegedly smuggled into Germany and was widespread among the German people. The document was intended to be construed falsely by the Germans as a Jewish blueprint for a New World Order. The document, in form, is almost identical to the eighteenth century *Protocols of the Illuminati*. That there is some ongoing conspiracy seems historically factual. That there are modicum of Jews involved is unquestionable. That it is confined to only a Jewish conspiracy is highly improbable.

Hitler incriminated and indicted a whole race of people because of a few Jews (the Rothschilds) who had joined a number of Gentile bankers and plunged the world into a sea of red ink. Hitler's fire of hatred and suspicion was reinforced when the Rothschilds proposed and backed the Zionist movement in Israel.

But there were multitudes of Jews living throughout Europe that were vehemently against a Jewish state. They were anti-Zionistic and opposed any state for the Jews. They argued that until Messiah came there should not be a place for the Jews— until their king had come there should be no kingdom.

The secrecy that has enshrouded the International Banking Cabal has allowed it to remain virtually unknown to the world as well as to world Jewry. Nonetheless, this banking elite seems to have a strong feeling toward Israel in that it was the Rothschilds who helped fund the reestablishment of the state of Israel. They were also behind the scenes setting the stage for the Balfour declaration.[4]

HITLER'S REACTION TO THE JEWS

Some have claimed that Karl Marx was a Jew. It is true that Marx's family was of Jewish descent, but his parents converted to Protestantism before Karl's birth.[5] Those who falsely claim that Marx was a Jew do so to add credence to the claim for the Jewish conspiracy theory. Karl Marx was baptized Protestant. Later in his life Marx turned from God and developed a hatred toward religion in any form. Marx was atheistic, denying the God of Judaism as well as the God of Christianity.

It was Karl Marx who instigated the philosophy of communism that was so destructive towards Germany's nation building in the 1850s and '60s. It is also true, however, in all fairness, that in the Russian Revolution there were apostate Jews who hated religion but had a politico-Zionism at heart. It is true that at the helm of the finances for this global world rule were the Rothschilds (formerly the Bauers), who were of Jewish background. This is what Hitler saw.[6]

Hitler's diabolical hatred toward the Jews stemmed from his perceptions that the Jews, as a people, sought to take over the whole world, and that the Rothschild-financed Bolshevik Revolution was another step toward that end. In many of his speeches he expressed this belief.

The following is from a German newspaper:

> On February 24, 1920, an ex-corporal in the German army named Adolf Hitler and a group of professional anti-Semitic agitators, including Julius Streicher, Alfred Rosenberg, and Gottfried Feder, met in a Munich beer hall and founded a new National Socialist Party.

The core of their National Socialist (Nazi) Party program was the racist doctrine that only those with German blood in their veins might be considered a citizen of Germany. Therefore, no Jew could belong to the German nation. The Nazis declared that anti-Semitism was the emotional foundation of their movement; every member of the Nazi Party was an anti-Semite.

Hitler, the Führer (dictatorial leader) of the Nazi Party, proudly announced his anti-Semitism as well as his inhumanity.

> Yes we are barbarians; we want to be barbarians; it is an honorable title. We shall rejuvenate the world; this

world is near its end. We are now near the end of the Age of Reason. The Ten Commandments have lost their validity. Conscience is a Jewish invention. It is a blemish, like circumcision. There is no such thing as truth, either in the moral or in the scientific sense. We must distrust the intelligence and the conscience and must place our trust in our instincts. And was not the whole doctrine of Christianity, with its faith in redemption, its moral code, its conscience, its conception of original sin, the outcome of Judaism?[7]

This last statement of Hitler's is the most revealing about the global conspiracy as he felt it related to the Jews.

The struggle for world domination will be fought between us, between Germans and Jews.

Adolf Hitler[8]

Hitler's own attempt at world dominion was essentially an attempt to break out of the grasp of the international banking elite.

CHAPTER SIXTEEN

The Satanic Resurrection

> And I saw one of his heads as it were wounded to
> death; and his deadly wound was healed: and all the
> whole world wondered after the beast.
>
> *Revelation 13:3*

Here in Revelation 13 is a resurrection of the seventh head which had been slain. The resurrection is actually mentioned three times. In Revelation 17 the resurrection is also mentioned.

> And the beast that was, and is not, even he is the
> eighth, and is of the seven.
>
> *Revelation 17:11*

These scriptures must be looked at together. How can chapter 13 show seven heads where the seventh is slain by a great sword and comes back to life, while in chapter 17 the resurrection of the seventh head is spoken of as an eighth, which comes out of the seven? Why didn't the Holy Spirit, who inspires all Scripture, say something like this: "I looked and saw the seventh head resurrected," and leave it at that? Why does he say in Revelation 17, "I saw an eighth head, which is of the seven"? What does this mean? Herein, we witness the beauty and precision of the Word of God. There can only be one answer to this question.

When the seventh head's fatal wound is healed, it comes back in a *different capacity* or *expanded form*. How can the totality of the Beast as represented by John's panoramic vision of the seven heads and ten horns (see Revelation 13), be concentrated into an eighth head? "And the beast that was, and is not, even he is the eighth, and is of the seven" (Revelation 17:11). It is because this eighth Global World Empire is the synthesis and totality of all the preceding empires combined and concentrated into one head, the eighth head.

In the past, many theologians and others believed that the slain head was a man. During the 1960s, many thought that John Kennedy would perhaps have a satanic resurrection and be the revived head or the Antichrist. But it is clear that the heads on the Beast are empires, and these empires are depicted in symbolic form.

The mystery of this scripture has stumped biblical scholars for centuries. Most of the missing information needed to solve this mystery was given in the last chapter, but there are some additional facts.

The death blow had to occur to fulfill prophecy. It was necessary for there to be a breakup of the limited world control by the British Empire. It is highly unlikely that the world planners anticipated the degree to which Hitler got out of hand. Certainly the war worked to their advantage because it ended British world control. It took two world wars to do it.

The Satanic Resurrection

Warfare, specifically global world war, greatly benefits the money brokers. They derive terrific economic advantage by the financing of both the military buildup and the urban renewal projects that come as a result of war's devastation. When the warring factions face the realities of rebuilding their countries, they must borrow large sums of money at usurious interest rates, thus bringing in great revenues to the international bankers.[1]

In this way money is further concentrated in the hands of a banking elite, and the nations are weakened and brought into submission through debt. By instigating the wars and backing both sides, the bankers can't possibly lose. They win from both sides.

> How art thou fallen from heaven, O Lucifer, son of the morning! how art thou cut down to the ground, which didst weaken the nations!
>
> *Isaiah 14:12*

Most historians agree that the two world wars of the last century were actually only one great war with several years of peace separating the two parts. If one were to study the elements that forged the beginning of World War I, it would be difficult to find a reason for why the whole world went to war in the first place. The fact of the matter is that there was no real cause for World War I to begin in 1914. Why then a war?

There were some interesting problems in Europe prior to the outbreak of hostilities in 1914. Europe could not afford to go to war simply because there was not enough mobilization of credit to enable the funding of the massive buildup necessary to finance such a venture.

The bankers in London solved the problem by contriving to set up a central banking system for the United States. Their agent, Paul Warburg, had been sent to develop the plan and have it formalized into law. The actual plan came to pass and became known as the Federal Reserve Act.[2] Late in 1913, the United States Congress passed this act, which Woodrow Wilson rubber-stamped, centralizing the bank of the United States of America, and thus mobilizing the credit of the industrial giant. This mobilization of credit established the loaning capability to finance the First World War.

Eventually the great world wars would bring to an end the seventh head of John's Beast, the British Empire. It was slain by a great sword, the world wars. Out of this would come the resurrected eighth head of the Beast, the final world empire.

> And here is the mind which hath wisdom. The seven heads are seven mountains, on which the woman sitteth. And there are seven kings: *five are fallen,* and one is, and the other is not yet come; and when he cometh, he must continue a short space. And the beast that was, and is not, even he is the eighth, and is of the seven, and goeth into perdition.
>
> *Revelation 17:9-11*

THE GREAT MIRACLE WORKER

The resurrection of the slain head (into the eighth head) is accomplished by the capacity and work of the second Beast, or *the False Prophet.* The False Prophet resurrects the seventh head. He is the builder of the last great world empire, which would also have ten horns, as spoken of by Daniel. The apostle John also saw ten horns on his rendition of the Beast. These horns are ten kings or kingdoms. While Daniel saw a little horn that proceeded out from the ten horns, John did not. This little horn grew larger than the ten horns (Daniel 7:20-24). This little horn that grows up larger (with the help of the False Prophet) than his ten compatriots seems to be the personification of a man who rules over the whole organism. The whole organism is encapsulated in John's vision as the eighth head that comes out of the seven (see Revelation 13).

The practical development of such a colossal edifice is by the effort of this second Beast. He finishes the age-old Beast system, bringing it to its final and completed form. In order for there to be an eighth head, the second Beast must be present and functioning, since it is through his effort that the New Global World Order will arise at the end of the age.

CHAPTER SEVENTEEN

The Agent of Antichrist

For two thousand years, Bible scholars have studied and wondered at the images of these two beasts of Revelation 13. Throughout the centuries, countless attempts have been made to identify each of these symbols as they relate to human history.

Now that we have moved through twenty centuries—some two thousand years since the birth of Christ—and six thousand years of recorded human history, most all the earth is expecting some kind of climactic event that will usher in the new millennium.

Since believers in Christ should be looking for His imminent return, those within the commonwealth of faith should be reading the news carefully. History's unfolding events point to a clear understanding of what, and who, these symbolic creatures (beasts) represent. The arising of both beasts are signs that precede the return of Jesus Christ. The believer should be awake, looking intently to bolster his precious faith, and seeking the encrypted meaning of the beast symbols.

The faithful are charged to warn the world of the coming judgment and to open the eyes of the blind with the good news of Christ's return. God intended His prophetic Word to shine in the darkness, enabling those with a willing heart to see clearly the approaching of the *day of the Lord*. While prophetic clarity tends to be fogged, the true disciples of Christ should be keen students of biblical prophecy.

THE UNITED NATIONS

After the end of the Second World War, and the accompanying end of the British Empire (the seventh kingdom slain by the sword), the world was asleep as the eighth head, an eighth kingdom, emerged like a Phoenix from the ashes of the ancient Roman Empire.

Scripture points out that this eighth head or empire will have ten kings or kingdoms combined in an alliance, and they will give their support to a world dictator. Scripture also teaches that this world dictator will be the False Christ, or the Antichrist (Daniel 7:7).

THE BEAST EMERGES FROM THE SEA

The Beast in Revelation 13 slowly emerges from the sea into full view. These verses show that the revealing of the Beast will be gradual. It *emerges* from the sea. It is somewhat unnoticed, but then comes into full view. In Daniel 8 we have a description of the little horn. First wee see the little horn *smaller* than its contemporaries.

> I considered the horns, and, behold, there came up
> among them *another little horn*...
>
> *Daniel 7:8 (emphasis added)*

Then we find that *it grows larger* than the ten horns, finally pulling three from their roots.

> And of the ten horns that were in his head, and of the
> other which came up, and before whom three fell; even
> of that horn that had eyes, and a mouth that spake very
> great things, *whose look was more stout [larger in
> appearance] than his fellows.*
>
> Daniel 7:20 (emphasis added)

Today, the only superpower left in the world is the United
States. A nation that was begun by a few folks who came over on
the Mayflower (from England, *the smallest of nations*) has grown
into the world's last and only superpower capable of uprooting
nations.

It seems clear that in these last moments of time there is no
other nation that can challenge America's preeminence in the
world today. Most likely, America is the little horn nation of
Daniel, and we shouldn't be remiss to keep our eye on the presidency of the United States.

When one stops to consider that the political apparatus for
a Global World Empire (the United Nations) was developed and
established here in the United States, the implications take on an
ominous tone. In addition, the UN's present location on
Manhattan Island in New York was bequeathed by the
Rockefeller family, prominent international bankers. This
makes the emerging Beast rising from the sea even more like an
elephant in the room—even to those that want to ignore its
presence. The ten kings, however, remain to be seen.

As believers in prophecy rivet their attention on the more
recent developments, they have inadvertently neglected the second Beast. There are two beasts mentioned in this very cryptic
section of Scripture.

WHAT ABOUT THE SECOND BEAST?

It has been a mystery that has lurked in the shadow of the
first Beast for thousands of years. Yet, it also appears at the end
of the age along with the Global World Empire, the first beast.

We now see the emerging Antichrist nation (United States)
and the suprastructure of a world political body (United

Nations) come into view, but what about the mysterious ten kings? What light do we have?

There are currently three possibilities:

1. The Common Market and its new monetary system (the Euro);
2. The Club of Rome's ten global federated economic zones;
3. The United States ten economic zones, set up under President Nixon.

As we see the eighth head emerging in these physical manifestations, the frightening reality is that the second Beast must be present on the earth. How so?

It is the second Beast whose function it is to advance and finish the final construction of the first Beast.

Few realize that it is the two-horned Beast, the second Beast, that is contemporary with the final stage of the first Beast, the agent of the Antichrist, and the architect who completes the entire Beast system.

If the rising of a One World Global Government epicentered in the United Nations (a revived Roman Empire) can be seen, then the second Beast must be in existence and functioning; it is he, according to Scripture, who finalizes the Beast system.

The question remains, who, and what, is pulling all this together? Who is this second Beast of Revelation 13:11? What is the identity of this mysterious second Beast?

CHAPTER EIGHTEEN

The False Prophet (the Second Beast)

There are hidden clues, which emerge from studying the first Beast, that begin to unlock the identity of the second Beast. A return to a view of the first Beast is vital in discovering these facts.

As most students of prophecy already know, the first Beast of Revelation is also mentioned in Daniel (chapters 7 and 8). There is a significant difference, however, between what Daniel saw in his vision and what the apostle John saw in his. Both saw a One World Government, but there was a difference in what each saw. In that difference lies the first key to unlock the mystery of the second Beast.

DANIEL'S VISION

Daniel had a preview of the future, looking forward from his time to the end of the world. He saw the last phase or manifestation of the Beast system composed of ten kings (Daniel 7:7).

He also saw a little horn, or king, with human eyes (Daniel 7:8). Daniel actually had a preview of the "man of lawlessness," the Antichrist. The Antichrist has also been called the world dictator who will control the ten nation confederacy. Daniel's vision was chronological—from his time forward, all the way to the last Global World Empire ruled by a man, the Antichrist.

John's View

John, on the other hand, saw panoramically. John, who lived in the first century, was given a total panoramic view of time. He was able to see from his time backward into history and forward into the future. His vision began with the Egyptian Empire (around 2500 B.C.) all the way through time to the last days, when the ten-horned kingdom that Daniel saw appears at the end of the age.

John saw a comprehensive panoramic and composite global *world system* that has been—and still is to this day—under construction, nearly five thousand years old (Revelation 13:1). Daniel merely saw the last form of that system in the last days, with the Antichrist coming to power at the end of time. John in his vision *does not give us any view of the Antichrist.*

This is not to say that John didn't believe in the Antichrist. He, too, knew of the man of sin, but his vision on the island of Patmos did not reveal the Antichrist, only the Beast system.

Since John clearly saw the first Beast as a system, the pronoun "he" in the scripture pertains to the *symbol* that represents the system of the Beast. It is not speaking of some person (i.e. the Antichrist). Rather, it pertains to the symbol: he, the Beast, the system; not he, the Beast, a man. Contextually, this gives us a precedent. The second Beast is also a system and not a person, as many have thought. Since the second Beast is called the False Prophet, theologians assume it to be a man. It should not be thought of as an actual human being simply because the pronoun "he" is used; neither should we anthropomorphize the symbolism simply because of the terminology "the False

Prophet." In the case of the second Beast as in the case of the first Beast, *the pronoun relates to the symbol, not to what the symbol represents.* (See the Appendix for more information on the False Prophet.)

To bring clarity to the function of the second Beast he (or it) has been tagged the False Prophet because this entity gives out a misrepresentation of a religious idea. *Pseudo prophetes* is Greek for "false prophet."[1] This simply means "false messenger."

LET THERE BE CLARITY

Let there be clarity. First, there will be a man of lawlessness called the Antichrist. Second, there will be the Beast, which is a Global World Government system controlled and run by the Antichrist. The Beast is not the Antichrist, and the Antichrist is not the Beast. Third, there will be the False Prophet, or the second Beast, which is also a system, *not a man.* The three are distinct, but they are all related in spirit to serve only one purpose: to bring about a Global World Government and the worship of Lucifer on the earth.

The second Beast shows up near the end of the age to finalize the construction of the New Global World Order, which includes the ten kings, and the setting up of the Antichrist. The False Prophet appears in time, *specifically, after the healing of a fatal wound* to one of the seven heads of the Beast as seen in Revelation 13:3.

The resurrected eighth head, evidenced in the United Nations, arose out of the slain British Empire, through the collaborative effort of England and the United States. The slain head has already been identified as the British Empire. The resurrected eighth head, the United Nations, came out of the seventh head, Great Britain in collaboration with the United States. The "little horn" of Daniel—which starts out smaller then grows larger than the ten kings, and eventually rules over the ten— seems to fit the historical development of the United States. It began with ninety people, and has become the only superpower on earth today. The little horn, by its description in symbolic language, appears to be the synthesis of both a nation state and a man. The most powerful political office in the world today is the presidency of the United States.

America fits that description, but we still wait to see who the embodiment of the horn is in a man. The ten kings are still yet future as well; they remain to be seen.

OLD TESTAMENT FORESHADOWS

Old Testament types are used in Scripture to foreshadow a New Testament fulfillment. For example, the Ark of the Covenant carried by the Jewish priests was a foreshadowing of the believer. The parting of the Red Sea when God delivered the Hebrews from Pharaoh was a type of water baptism. The serpent raised in the wilderness was a foreshadowing of the cross. Jesus was the fulfillment of the Old Testament Passover lamb sacrificed by the Jews when they were slaves in Egypt.

Nevertheless, finding and Old Testament foreshadowing of the second Beast of Revelation 13 presents difficulties. The first Beast of Revelation is clearly foreshadowed in Daniel, and later John gives more light and detail on the subject. However, the second Beast is not so easily seen in the Old Testament.

There are some clues. John's vision of the first Beast *as a system* sets the tone and context for the interpretation of the second Beast as a system, but we must dig deep for two more clues concerning the identity of the second Beast.

THE TWO HORNS

> And I beheld another beast coming up out of the earth; and he had *two horns*...
>
> *Revelation 13:11 (emphasis added)*

Scripture interprets Scripture, and it does not change to suit our conjectural whims. Since the Scripture cannot change and is consistent throughout, if horns represent kings in one place, *horns must represent kings in all places* throughout apocalyptic Scripture.

> The ram which thou sawest having *two horns* are the kings of Media and Persia.
>
> *Daniel 8:20 (emphasis added)*

If horns, as has been indicated, represent kings or kingdoms, the Beast with *two horns* in Revelation 13 represents two kings or two kingdoms *that combine to make a system* that is called the False Prophet.

It has been said that there is vague reference in the Old Testament to shed light on the second Beast in Revelation 13. It also can be said that the two nations of Media and Persia as a two-horned beast in Daniel 8:3 lays down an Old Testament precedent for a two-nation alliance depicted in symbolism as a two-horned beast.

Interpreting the False Prophet as a solitary man would *not* take into consideration the two horns in light of biblical precedents. *The false prophet is an alliance of two kingdoms.* It is a system (the False Prophet in the lake of fire—see Appendix).

"And he had two horns like a lamb, and he spake as a dragon" (Revelation 13:11). In the Old Testament, the Scripture as recorded through the prophet Daniel describes the Gentile world powers as beasts. The figurative language Daniel uses to describe the ruling powers actually contains the characteristics of those ruling nations.

For example, Daniel saw the Babylonian Empire as a lion, the king of the jungle. This indicated the regal power of Nebuchadnezzar and the greatest of all civilizations. He saw the second empire as a bear, which described the characteristics of the Medes and Persians. The Medo-Persian Empire was known for its sheer power and weight in numbers of people. The Grecian Empire he characterized as a leopard, cunning and swift, always stalking the prey and moving quickly over the land. This is exactly how Alexander the Great operated. The fourth beast, Rome, was different than the others. It seemed to be a mechanical and heartless system.

These little cameos of the former empires in symbolic form are mentioned here only to bring light and embellishment upon the imagery and interpretation of the second Beast, as it is also described in symbolic form.

THE LAMB-LIKE APPEARANCE OF THE FALSE PROPHET

The second Beast is described as lamb-like in appearance. A lamb in the Bible is first mentioned in the life of Abel (Genesis 4:4).

The age-old story records that when Abel went to worship he took a lamb from his flock and sacrificed it to the Lord. This sacrifice was acceptable to the Lord, and it was a foreshadowing of Christ, the Lamb of God.

When God was testing Abraham's obedience, He required a lamb as a substitutionary sacrifice for Abraham's son Isaac (Genesis 22:8). The ancient Jews were also required to sacrifice a lamb and paint the blood of the lamb on the lintel of the door, escaping the judgment that was coming down on Egypt (Genesis 12:3; Exodus 12:21-23). In all these cases, a lamb was a foreshadowing of Christ.

The False Prophet, or the second Beast, is false because it represents itself as Christ-like (thus, the characterization as a lamb). Yet, in reality, underneath the veneer it is satanic—it speaks like a dragon, a wolf in sheep's clothing.

Remember, this second Beast is a two-nation alliance, or system. If the lamb symbol is a Christian symbol, then the two kingdoms, or horns, represent *two Christian nations*, or two nations that are at least *considered* Christian nations: They have a Christian pretense or appearance, but underneath it resides a darkness. The fact that it "speaks as a dragon" explains that beneath the Christian pretense hides the devil: a liar, a thief, and a murderer.

The second Beast, then, is a system of two alleged Christian nations joined to form an alliance, who by their external appearance (look like a lamb, i.e., Christian) give out a deceiving message or impression. What two nations, which have banded together to build a One World Global System for the seat of Antichrist, could this be talking about? Before this question can be answered there are additional facts that must be uncovered.

THE SPHERE OF AUTHORITY OF THE FALSE PROPHET

> And he exerciseth all the power of the first beast before
> him, and causeth the earth and them which dwell
> therein to worship the first beast, whose deadly wound
> was healed.
>
> *Revelation 13:12*

This section of Scripture is critical in destroying vain speculations concerning the identity of the False Prophet. Hopefully the Scripture by itself will bury those annoying conjectures.

The key words are "he" and "all": "*he* exercises *all* the authority of the first Beast." This statement is very revealing. One must ask the very important question, "If the False Prophet exercises *all* the authority of the first Beast, just what is the extent of the authority of the first Beast?"

The word "authority" used here is the Greek word *exousia*, which means "legislative authority" or "licensing authority."[2] The False Prophet has all the licensing authority of the first Beast. This is a great deal more than mere religious authority, as we shall see. Just what is (and has been) the comprehensive authority of this five-thousand-year-old Beast system?

The Beast with the ten horns—and the seven heads, as you will recall—was a symbolic representation of all the empires that controlled the world from the time of the Egyptians to this present day. The fundamental controlling authority of those empires worked over the spheres of politics, economics, law, military, education, and, to a great degree, religion.

Think of the power of Egypt, Babylon, Greece, and Rome. Think of the British Empire and its navy, its commercial life, its state-run religion, and its banking power. The False Prophet operates with *all* the power of the first Beast: all the authority and power, all the spheres and dimensions of an empire.

Think of the power he wields. How would it be to have *all power* over the Western world's political, economic, legal, military, educational, and religious areas of life?

The important point to be made here, in no uncertain terms, is that this is not just some religious entity moving with a new religious order of some sort. The False Prophet's power extends far beyond the sphere of the religious dimension. This Beast moves with *all* authoritative power.

HE IS CONTEMPORARY

> And he exerciseth all the power of the first beast *before him [in his presence]*.
>
> *Revelation 13:12 (emphasis added)*

The phrase "in his presence" shows us that the two entities are contemporary—that they appear together—but the authority of the False Prophet has not been received from the first Beast. It seems as though both of the two entities have the same authoritative power source. The first Beast is apathetic towards the authority of the False Prophet; he doesn't seem to be intimidated by the False Prophet's power. They work together to produce the final result.

In a moment we shall see the operation of the False Prophet's comprehensive authority. These facts are important because they help us acquire a greater objectivity about just who and what the False Prophet is.

To recapitulate the facts of the False Prophet:

1. The second Beast is a two-horned system, or a two-nation confederacy.
2. He will function during a period when the seventh head of the first Beast has been healed from a fatal wound of war (a great sword). He is contemporary with the first Beast's last phase of completion.
3. He will have *all* the power of the first Beast.

The False Prophet also does great signs:

1. He will have power to call fire down from heaven.
2. He will be able to deceive the whole world, particularly through an image.
3. He will abolish all economic systems where cash is used as the medium of exchange and introduce a cashless system that will operate through 666 (see Revelation 13:12-18).

These great signs and wonders that the second Beast performs will be dealt with in more detail in later chapters, but all these great powers are at his disposal to finalize the construction of the last great Global World System.

It is a great mistake to assign to the False Prophet the small task of merely building a new, worldwide religion. As we have shown, his power extends far beyond religious deception.

WHEN SHALL THESE THINGS BE?

Today, many believe that these manifestations of the powers of the second Beast will occur at a point in the future. Could it be that they are already in operation today?

The discussion of this topic will cause great pain to many people. It calls into question one's presuppositional position on biblical prophecy (eschatology—the study of last things) and, therefore, one's approach to the book of Revelation.

LOOKING AT REVELATION

Basically there are four known schools of thought for the interpretation of the book of Revelation.

1. The spiritual scheme: The Apocalypse is given to teach fundamental spiritual principles.
2. The preterist scheme: The book only teaches events taking place on earth during the Roman era, during the time of the apostle John's lifetime.
3. The historic scheme: The symbols in Revelation relate to events in the history of the world that are relevant to the welfare of the church from the first century to modern times.
4. The futurist scheme: This view insists that, for the most part, the visions of the book will be future, toward the end of the age.

The question one has to ask is, which of the above positions is accurate? That is, which set of spectacles should be used?

There has been constant debate on this problem for hundreds of years, and the believer is left to ferret it out for himself. Each point of view has its merits. In the North American church, the prominent view is, by and large, the futurist scheme.

The futurist scheme, for the most part, insists that the visions of Revelation will be fulfilled toward the end of the age. While there may be a great deal of truth to this position, it also creates its own problem. The problem with "futurism" is that the closer we move toward the end of the age, the more likely we are to overlook and miss the events predicted in the symbols and assign their fulfillment to some future time. This view keeps pushing the fulfillment of events ahead into the future so that we never arrive.

This is not to say that history should conform to our conjectural whims simply because we are impatient for the fulfillment of prophecy. However, the Lord also clearly said, "But ye, brethren, are not in darkness, that the day should overtake you as a thief" (1 Thessalonians 5:4).

A careful study of history will show that the False Prophet has been with us for some time, and that he is alive and in the world today.

CHAPTER NINETEEN

History of the False Prophet— the New Zion

For most of them, it began as an escape from feudalism and the despotism that reigned over their religious lives. England and Europe were basically without a middle class. The average person had no hope of ever holding land. All property was considered owned by the king and was controlled by the very rich. The rest of the people were serfs.[1] This was called feudalism. In England the reigning king also dictated the nature of worship to God. Christianity was tightly controlled by the sovereign king.[2]

Those in England who continued to dream of freedom deeply desired a fresh start. They were willing to brave the difficulties and harshness of the journey to the New World. The ones that finally did venture out believed they were coming to the New Jerusalem, the promised land. The escape from England was looked at as an exodus from an Egypt, but they also viewed their awaited liberties in the new land with a prophetic sense of purpose.[3]

A Fresh Start

These visionaries had first-hand knowledge of the terrible bondage of feudalism and despotism. They saw the possibility in the new land as the potential fulfillment of all their hopes and dreams—a new nation (America) based upon the Judeo-Christian law and morality from the sacred Scriptures. In the beginning there was a terrible price to be paid as they carved out a niche in the hostile world, but, to them, it was a small price as they considered the great opportunity and the potential that lay before them.[4]

The Exodus

It started out as resistance to the Anglican Church. Religious oppression under the state-run church eventually became so intolerable that those who had deep-seated convictions about God had to leave. They were the separatists, and they moved across the English Channel to the mainland of Europe, to a place of refuge in Holland. After spending eleven years there, in exile from England, the hearts of the zealots still longed for a new freedom. The exhausting toil of eighteen-hour workdays for meager wages was straining their sensibilities. Why not break free and move to the New World in America?[5]

As a devout and religious people, they took council through corporate prayer. They believed that their God was inspiring them to brave the elements and trust Him for a new beginning in a far away land.[6] About a hundred of them crowded into the Mayflower—a ship roughly the size of a volleyball court—and for sixty-six days braved the awesome power of the mighty Atlantic Ocean.[7]

One year after landing at Plymouth Rock, almost half of the valiant band had starved to death. The Thanksgiving celebration later that year was the beginning of an American tradition memorializing their heroic faith in God.[8]

The lords of England on the other side of the Atlantic Ocean viewed the colonists as rebels. Like Pharaoh of Egypt, they would not let the people go to the land of promise without contest. Elitist elements within Britain sought to retain control and subdue the colonies. The new land, it was reasoned, must be kept under British control.[9]

THE BANK OF ENGLAND

In 1692, Massachusetts opened a mint and began to issue its own coins and, later, paper notes. These notes were considered full legal tender. The notes could be borrowed at low interest rates by the citizens for all sorts of needs: business, homes, etc. The revenues that came from these low-interest loans were used for public purposes and thus kept taxes down. This was all done without the consent of England. Other colonies followed the lead of Massachusetts and enjoyed great prosperity. The colonies paid no interest and therefore were not indebted to anyone.[10]

In England, however, King William III made a decision to give William Paterson and his associates a charter to establish a private bank. It was called the Bank of England.[11]

The king needed money to finance his war with France. This favor was extended in exchange for the loan. The bank had the exclusive privilege of issuing paper money and lending it at interest. With control of London and England's monetary system in hand, the bankers then fixed their gaze on the New World, intensely motivated and determined to control its currency as well.[12]

By 1720, every colonial governor was instructed to stop issuing their own paper notes. The bankers in England slyly used the British Board of Trade as their front, thus manipulating the Parliament and affecting decisions so that the English government would back their movements against the American colonies. The colonies refused to submit. The conflict that later boiled over and became the American Revolution was under way, but the seed of that armed conflict was the control of money.[13]

During 1767, Ben Franklin tried to fiscally conciliate the colonies with the Crown Empire, but Franklin's diplomacy did not work. While Franklin was in England, former Prime Minister Granville spoke to the House of Commons. His words became the guidance system for international banking.

> I will tell the honorable gentlemen of a revenue that
> will produce something valuable in America. Make
> paper money for the colonies [under British control],
> issue it upon loan there, take the interest and apply it as
> you think proper.[14]

Since the English government also held this underhanded vision it backed the Bank of England to the hilt. Therefore, the bank was ready to apply and enforce their policy of monetary control over the American colonies.

It should be crystal clear that the intent of this policy was to enslave the New World in and through debt. The colonies resisted this fiscal tyranny and met on June 10, 1775. There they resolved to create two million dollars in bills of credit that the united colonies would honor. This action was viewed by the British as open defiance and rebellion. The boiling point had been reached. The explosive social condition erupted in what came to be known as the Boston Tea Party. This was the event that launched the revolutionary war; the momentum for the war, however, had begun building some eighty years earlier.[15]

THE BOSTON TEA PARTY

The Boston Tea Party and the American Revolution expressed the deeply entrenched sentiments of those who yearned to be free from the domination of the British Empire. What the patriots were saying, as they dumped the tea into Boston Harbor, was that they were fed up with being taxed, fed up with having no control of their own credit, and fed up with the struggle over the printing of their own nation's money.[16]

Through taxation, the Americans essentially were paying to be policed by a power they didn't want ruling over them. This was their initial reason for the exodus from Britain. The British had cunningly extorted from the colonies money that was being used to garrison British troops on American soil. They did this to maintain a watchful eye on the colonies. The war for independence was over a whole lot more than a little tax on tea.

Although the escape to the New World was, to a great extent, a religious matter, the Revolutionary war was fought over taxation and, more importantly, who would control capital in the New World.

THE ROTHSCHILDS

The Rothschilds, a family of Jewish lineage, were very shrewd in their dealings with money. They gained large sums of capital by investment and later became international bankers. Five sons of Rothschild dispersed to continental Europe and set up banking houses in strategic locations in various European countries.[17]

Around 1799, the Rothschilds, with increased financial power, allied themselves with the Masonic secret societies. Under cover of obscurity they successfully destabilized the European continent by financing the French Revolution. London became the seat of the Rothschilds' international banking dynasty.[18]

The Rothschilds and other banking families were secretly establishing new power centers, as the dynastic monarchies of Europe were disintegrating. The influence of the bankers was exerted on both businesses and governments.[19]

The fledgling America presented an obstacle to the schemes for British world control held by the monetary interests. The new nation continued to refuse the shackles of a central bank, and America's credit remained relatively free from foreign control. Since lending power in America was not in the hands of the international manipulators, the bankers were frustrated in proceeding with their global aspirations.[20]

The fundamental concept these international pirates used in their business practice came from an promise in the Old Testament, which they twisted in their application to themselves. "Thou shalt lend unto many nations, but thou shalt not borrow; and thou shalt reign over many nations, but they shall not reign over thee" (Deuteronomy 15:6).

The Rothschilds built on this principle, but they subverted the scriptural intent and, instead, lent money at usurious rates. They believed that if they controlled the wealth of a nation, they could transcend and usurp the legal and political power of the state. Rothschild would often boast, "I care not who makes the laws of a nation, give me the wealth of a nation and I'll make the laws."[21] They conducted themselves along the lines of the blueprint for world control mapped out in the *Protocols of the Illuminati*.[22]

ADAM WEISHAUPT—THE ILLUMINATI

Adam Weishaupt was a professor of considerable renown at Ingolstadt University. He was driven by an incredible, diabolical ambition to rule the world. Unlike others throughout history who sought the same prize, Weishaupt was not a crude gangster sort who could lead a band of thieves and rowdies. Neither was he a military type who sought conquest through sheer force. Weishaupt was an intellectual, a professor at law. His high-minded self-conceit caused him to believe he was mentally superior to others. He was received into the Masonic Order of his day, where he found like-minded comrades.[23]

Those who banded together with Weishaupt felt they were of such superior fiber that they should be running the world. A secret order was devised called the Illuminati, which would become the vehicle for world conquest.[24]

THE SCOPE OF THE ILLUMINATI

The Order of the Illuminati sought to unite men from all places, all social classes, and all religions, despite the diversity of their opinions and passions. The idea was to make them *love the common interest of unity* and bond to the point where, together or alone, they act as one individual. The ultimate objective was to bring happiness to the world. The philosophy behind this was the rather novel idea that the end—happiness for the people—justified the means.[25]

The ultimate purpose of the Illuminati, however, was to take over the world. Talent for the Order was processed by an elaborate system of initiation. The initiate would have to pass from one degree to the next, with the goal being the completion of all the steps to full enlightenment. Weishaupt carefully plotted each step of the way, making sure the weakest would not rise above the lowest levels of the Order. The bold, ruthless, and cynical were brought along to the highest levels of Reagent, Magus, and Rex.[26]

ILLUMINISM AND FREEMASONRY

Weishaupt believed that his organization needed a cover and a way to extend its power. In 1782, he successfully infiltrated the Masonic Order with Illuminism at the congress of Wilhelmsbad.[27]

In America, George Washington, who was a Freemason, became aware of the movements of the Illuminati within the Masonic Order. A Christian minister gave Washington a book entitled *Proofs of a Conspiracy.* This was Washington's response to the book.

> It was not my intention to doubt that the doctrines of
> the Illuminati, and principles of Jacobinism, had not
> spread to the United States. On the contrary, no one is
> more fully satisfied of this fact than I am. The idea that
> I meant to convey was that I did not believe the Lodges
> of Freemasonry in this country had, as societies,
> endeavored to propagate the diabolical tenets of the
> Illuminati.[28]

For the Order to gain its objective, it was necessary to abolish religion, governments, and private property. The Order deemed these the real obstacles to true happiness. This is exactly what the Communists have been advocating since 1848. But most importantly, the Illuminati, and later the Communists, advocated the centralization of credit in the hands of the state by means of a national bank with state capital and an exclusive monopoly.[29]

In Europe, the Order of the Illuminati was driven underground when its plans were discovered. However, the ideas, the plans, and the goals—of John Ruskin, Cecil Rhodes, Rothschild, the Round Table, the CFR, the Bilderbergers, and Masonry—have lived on in the Communist movement.

THE BRITISH SPY SYSTEM

The British never conceded America's declared independence as the final inning in British world hegemony. Their aims of world dominion would not be frustrated by a few farmers and wild eyed dreamers on the other side of the Atlantic.

In the late eighteenth century in the United States, two prominent political figures squared off in a duel to the death. The gun fight is but a faint memory in the minds of most observers of history, but the reasons for the hostilities between these two famous historic personalities lays buried in the rubble of time. The battle to the death involved Alexander Hamilton, the father of the American banking system, and Aaron Burr, vice president of the United States.[30]

The story is somewhat a mystery, but it provides a key in unlocking important facts concerning Great Britain's continuous struggle to regain control of America. America's economic development is directly related to Britain's attempts to seize this nation. Through this study it can be seen why today the citizens of this land are buried in mountainous debt and thus monumental taxation: They are the same issues that brought about the American Revolution in the first place.

Since it was costly and difficult to maintain a war effort in the Western world—especially with Europe in turmoil from the outburst of the French Revolution—the British intelligence sent spies into the United States with the intent of seizing the country from within.

Their chief man of the hour was Rothschild's agent, Aaron Burr. Burr was a fully-trained agent of the British internationalists. Most importantly, Burr was a Scottish Rite Freemason of the 33rd degree. (The Illuminati infiltrated Scottish Rite Freemasonry.) Here, in the person of Aaron Burr, can be seen the synthesis of the intent of both the world bankers and the Illuminati Scottish Rite Freemasonry.[31]

After becoming governor of New York, Burr helped obtain cheap loans for the internationalists to buy up most of New York state. Burr helped found the Manhattan Bank (the Chase Manhattan Bank—now the J.P. Morgan Chase Manhattan Bank), and much has been written about his nefarious dealings in the South as he helped lay the groundwork for the Civil War in the first decade of the 1800s.[32]

When Burr sought to become president of the United States he was frustrated by Alexander Hamilton, who viewed him as a traitor. Burr was also highly suspected by George Washington. History documents Burrs family ties with Benedict Arnold, the most infamous traitor in American history.[33]

When he ran for president, Burr was narrowly defeated by Jefferson. Had it not been for Hamilton, the Rothschilds' agent would have become president of the United States of America. There is much behind the duel that most history books do not tell us, but the most important fact is yet to come.

THE BANK OF THE U.S.A.

Alexander Hamilton is known today as the father of the American banking system. Even though Hamilton was a red-blooded American, he wanted a central bank (modeled after the French ideal). The French ideal was simply that certain prominent, successful, and intelligent men would control the affairs of the bank. Jefferson was against the charter of such a bank, fearing too much power in the hands of an elitist group. Even though these men were Americans, Jefferson felt it was too dangerous a proposition.

Burr also wanted a central bank, but his bank would have internationalists as the ones in command. Burr killed Hamilton and fled to Britain. At issue was who would control money in the New World, the British banking system or an American group.

While Burr was vice president, he and Albert Gallatin (another internationalist, who had become secretary of the treasury) successfully sold the idea of the need for a balanced budget to Congress. By cutting military expenditures for the maintenance of the U.S. Navy, the defenses of the United States were weakened. This undermining of U.S. defenses opened the door for the British to stage another conflict.[34]

The second revolutionary war (in 1812) was orchestrated by the Trojan Horse of the British spy system that had infiltrated American politics. The second revolutionary war should have ended what Europeans called "the American experiment," but, to the exasperation of the British, the war failed. There is no explanation for America's survival except as an intervention of providence.[35]

THE CIVIL WAR: A BATTLE WITH THE BANKERS

By the time Abraham Lincoln became president, the United States had survived two revolutionary wars with Great Britain, as well as many political intrigues, especially during Andrew Jackson's administration. The pesky child nation, America, was causing great delay to the global aspirations of the British Empire. After the failure to recharter the bank of the United States, the European bankers began plotting another war.

During Lincoln's administration, the British inspired the Civil War. The war would create the need to finance the war through borrowing. The plotters realized the American people would not accept a national bank without a reason for having one. They decided upon a war. Wars are costly, and they force governments into a position in which they must borrow to finance the effort.

Who could the plotters induce to fight a war with America? Since America had become such a powerful nation, there was no one to rival her in the western hemisphere. No one.

The bankers made the decision to divide the nation into two parts, thereby creating an enemy from within the United States. The overt issue for the war was slavery, but the actual reason behind the Civil War was the splitting of the Union. The deeper motive was, of course, to seize control of the country by creating the financial need to borrow from the bankers at usurious interest rates, thus creating the need for a centralized bank.[36]

The whole story of the secession of the southern states was given by George L. Bickley, who declared that he created the fateful war of 1861. He worked through an organization called the Knights of the Golden Circle, which engineered and spread secession.[37]

INTERNATIONAL BANKERS LENDING CONTROL

The British bankers at that time also controlled the fledgling American banks, which offered to loan Abraham Lincoln money to fight the war. Lincoln wisely refused and created the famous Lincoln greenbacks with which he financed the Civil War.[38]

Abraham Lincoln, in a famous address, declared:

> At what point, then, is the approach of danger to be
> expected? I answer, if it ever reach us it must spring up
> among us, it cannot come from abroad. If destruction
> be our lot, we must ourselves be its author and finisher.
> As a nation of free men we must live through all time
> or die of suicide.[39]

Lincoln's refusal to finance the Union through debt to the internationalists demonstrated his keen insight into their strategy for global dominion. Hence, he financed the Civil War by printing the Lincoln greenbacks.

In both respects—with regard to the Civil War and the British banker's attempt to seize control of the economics of America—once again the aims of the globalists were frustrated. This is what caused Lincoln's assassination.

Nonetheless, America remained in control of her own credit. The result of this victory was low interest loans for entrepreneurs, which led to great business expansion.

This great expansion in the post-Civil War era enhanced the fears of those who sought to bring the world into a One World Order. If America was allowed to continue to expand, she would be a major—perhaps insurmountable—obstacle in the way of their goal.

For one hundred years, America was able to avoid total control of her capital by the international bankers. Lincoln was most certainly a great irritant to the aspirations of the globalists. He was the last president to seek categorically a halting of the globalists drive toward a Global One World Government. It cost him his life; he was murdered by John Wilkes Booth, an agent of the internationalists.[40]

America's emergence from the Civil War as a great industrial power was due to the effective centralization of capital and credit within the Federal Government, thanks to Lincoln. It was America's control over her own capital that was making her prosperous. It was the aim of the international bankers to change all that.

Lincoln was the victim of a major conspiracy—a conspiracy so important that even the European bankers were involved. Lincoln had to be eliminated because he dared to oppose their attempt to force a central bank on the United States. He became an example to those who would later oppose such machinations in high places. Could it be that, one hundred years later, John F. Kennedy was also a victim of this same intrigue?

CHAPTER TWENTY

History of the False Prophet— the Post-Civil War Era

I t became crystal clear to the globalists, after the American Civil War, that America had to be stopped. Frederick Engels, the British industrialist, was one of many who felt that the war would be the end of the American republic. The victory of the North proved him wrong. Now, the tremendous threat of the American system loomed an even greater shadow over the vast British Empire and continental Europe. A more vigorous strategy was plotted and pursued to finally overthrow England's rebellious child, now almost one hundred year old.

A plan to counter the great American expansion had to be conceived. A new economic warfare would be waged. The plan for this overthrow centered on the nation's money and credit. This was done by forces inside the United States contracting U.S. currency (greenbacks) and lowering tariff barriers so that

American markets could be exploited. Low tariffs meant that American industry would not be protected from foreign competition. This clandestinely contrived free trade policy would exploit the markets of America and suck money away from circulation in the States. In other words, in the eyes of the British, the greenbacks had to go because they kept the bankers from being in control.

Then, the international pirates sought to bring about reform by replacing industry builders with foreign agents in seats of economic and political power. In order to conquer America, her financial sovereignty must, of necessity, come to an end. This became the sole front of the internationalists in their pursuit for a One World Global Government.[1]

ENGLISH ECONOMIC COUNTER ATTACK

The internationalists refused to be deterred. Neither the Revolution, nor the second revolutionary war, nor the failure of the rechartering of the bank, nor the failure of the Civil War could frustrate their aspirations. They never ceased to work to subjugate and recapture America. However, a new strategy was planned. The British intelligence, under the control of the internationalists, sought to undermine the new nation from deep within.

Conspirators were sent to the United States to assail the greenbacks. The English-backed Golden Club was implanted in the eastern United States for the sole purpose of throttling the successes of Lincoln's economic policies. After much wrangling and dissimulation, restrictions were placed upon the greenbacks.[2]

The bankers fought hard against the American government's attempt to recapture its own credit and money. They emerged from their war on Lincoln's greenbacks with the prize. The restrictions that were placed upon the greenbacks caused a perception that made them inflationary. The bankers, with clever manipulation, were able to expand and contract the economy. They would not accept the greenbacks in payment for lands they had bought from the government. They demanded gold. For many years there was a general looting of the government's gold, and the huge banking house of J.P. Morgan was built as an international banking island upon the American soil.[3]

During the administration of Abraham Lincoln, the powerful London-based banking house of Rothschild was behind the efforts to throttle the control of—and to seize—credit and money in America. In a letter to Mr. Belmont, Rothschild warned of ruin for those who might oppose the payment of U.S. bonds in coin or who might advocate their liquidation in greenbacks.[4]

IDEOLOGICAL ECONOMIC WAR AND POLITICAL INTRIGUE

Frederick Engels

Frederick Engels was a brilliant British industrialist whose business depended greatly on cheap American slave cotton. Engels, who was the most famous of all British industrialists, paid great homage to the East India House think tank. The mind trust included men like Thomas Carlyle, John Stuart Mill, Thomas Malthus, and Charles Darwin—all of whom had great influence on Engels. Their political economic socialist ideas, based upon feudalism, became Engels' launching pad for his development of the ideology of communism. Frederick Engels was the founder of Marxist communism and author of its doctrine. He was personal mentor of Karl Marx.

What was most greatly feared by the British internationalists was beginning to truly threaten their plans for entire global control. America and her nation-building Republican system was being brought to the mainland of Europe by Germany. It was being accomplished by Frederick List, who had been sent to America to study the American system.[5]

List, after watching the success of the American republican model, believed it was his duty and responsibility to promote everything that may increase the wealth and power of *the nation*. Tariffs must be erected to protect fledgling industry from nations that would attempt to loot by bringing cheaper goods. List saw the evil of free trade.[6]

The British imperial system was the antithesis of this. Those in control knew the advantages of a free trade system and its power to maintain both the expansion of its own economy and overall world control.

As the thrust of the American system's influence grew and was introduced to Germany, a secret British offensive was launched against these neo-German republicans and Abraham Lincoln's economic program in the United States.

It was in 1843 that Frederick Engels, father of communism, entered the fray. In his first treatise on economics, he attacked Christianity (the base of the American republican system) and carefully directed his readers to the free trade versus protectionist battle then going on in Germany. He pointed out how essential it was to follow the position of free trade as the "proper course of action" and "the shorter road to wealth."[7]

Engels, after winning over Karl Marx, published their first co-authored book, *The Condition of the Working Class*. The book served as a false prophetic warning to the German working class of the horrors in store for them if (energized by America) imported industrialization developed.[8]

Marx then teed off on Frederick List through his book *The National System of Political Economy*; he branded List as a propagator of the special interests of German manufacturers.

The titanic battle between the ideologies of republicanism and feudalism stymied the industrialization and unification of Germany until the latter part of the nineteenth century. As the Engels/Marx communist duet was gaining the upper hand in slowing the growth of mainland European industrialization, they used the same fear inspired by these literary weapons for international globalism.

Lincoln's greenbacks mobilized national credit in America and thus financed the victory of the North in the Civil War. Had Lincoln surrendered to the temptation of the bankers' loans (with exorbitant interest rates), the borrower (the U.S.A.) would have become slave to the lender (England). Lincoln saw the evils of both the free trade ideology and the slavery system that supported cheap cotton for England's textile mills, which allowed them to maintain a tremendous economic edge over the rest of the world.[9]

Britain, in control of raw materials, could bring the cotton to England, then sell it back as finished products at high profit not only in America but all over the world. If ever these nations were to industrialize and manufacture their own finished products, they could erect trade barriers and destroy the monopoly that the British enjoyed over these worldwide markets.

Here the ideological mixture of communism and British free trade expansionism was the not-so-strange brew that was created to stifle the Christian based republicanism of American design. As a result, it successfully stifled the advancement of industrialization to the European continent, which could have enabled nations to break out of feudalist indentured slavery.[10]

The Communist movement was one of a number of political weapons created by British strategists to counter the spread of the tremendously successful American system to the European continent.

BRITAIN'S CONQUEST OF MAMMON

The Rothschilds' War Chest for Globalism

In the late nineteenth and early twentieth centuries, with the American purse falling more and more into the hands of the international banking elite, the final conflict to set up the hundred-year-old Illuminati plan for an American central bank was staged.

As the internationalists orchestrated the depression of 1907, the American populace was finally psychologically prepared to receive a centralized banking plan, a plan that promised to control and stabilize the flow of capital. The plan called for a central bank that was promised to be run by the government. It would be a bank that would regulate cash flows with the promise that there would never again be a shortage of money in circulation. It would insure that there would always be sufficient money, the life blood of an economy, flowing in the economy.[11]

Great Deception

The international planners knew—oh, how they knew—that the American people would never accept a plan that could possibly allow private interests to control the bank. The American people wanted a bank that was controlled by the government, not by private banking houses like the Rothschilds and the J.P. Morgans.

> I care not who makes the laws of the nations. Give me
> the wealth of the nations and I'll make the laws.
>
> *Rothschild*[12]

Under a cloak of great secrecy, the plotters of world financial and governmental control retreated to a place called *Jekyll Island*. There they plotted and schemed and created, with great subtlety, the Federal Reserve Act. The Rothschilds sent their special agent, Paul Warburg, to head up the delegation. His mission was to stage the takeover and set up the American banking system.

Jekyll Island

Warburg called together the most powerful and wealthy families in America. Then, with their support, he drafted two infamous plans that laid the groundwork for the seizure of the American banking system. Actually, there was just one plan with two different names. At Jekyll Island, the representatives of these powerful families made agreements that framed the diabolical plot. Plan one was called the Aldrich Plan. Plan two was called the Federal Reserve Act. History records which one of these identical plans was accepted by the U.S. Congress.[13]

The Federal Reserve

The Federal Reserve Act created what became the central bank of the United States of America: the Federal Reserve System.

Contrary to popular understanding, the Fed is *not* controlled by the U.S. government but by representatives who are selected by the international bankers themselves.[14] The Fed's decision making processes reminds one of the fox who guarded the chicken house. Unbeknownst to the American public, the Federal Reserve System is a private corporation that in 1913, by craft and guile, became the American banking system. Actually, the name Federal Reserve was given for the express purpose of deceiving the populace into thinking it was a government agency. It is not.[15]

George Washington, the father of his country, spoke these words of wisdom concerning the formation of a central bank.

> Shall a few designing men, for their own aggrandizement, and to glorify their own avarice, overset the goodly fabric we have been rearing at the expense of much time, blood and treasure?[16]

Father George saw the evil desire of the international bankers and what they sought to accomplish with a central bank. This statement by George Washington caused the founding fathers to carefully craft into the Constitution to the United States Congress the specially assigned powers of Congress to include:

> Congress shall have the power to coin money and regulate the value thereof.[17]

The purpose of this delegation of authority to Congress was to specifically prevent robbery and exploitation of the American money system by a select few. The Federal Reserve Act was passed on December 23, 1913; Woodrow Wilson refused to veto the passage of the bill by Congress. It took away the legal authority of Congress—and thus the American people—the power to coin or print money, and it gave this power to a private printing company called the Federal Reserve. Basically, what this meant was that the Fed could print money and charge interest. The revenues derived from that interest would accrue to the personal benefit of the principal stock holders of the Federal Reserve (corporation) System.

This is exactly what Thomas Jefferson feared, what Abraham Lincoln opposed, and what George Washington warned of. The victory for which the founding patriots gave their lives during the revolutionary war had been simply handed over to those they so valiantly fought against.

The Federal Reserve Act was passed on December 23, 1913, while most of the Congress was home for Christmas. But what did the plan allow for? The very thing Aaron Burr sought one hundred years earlier: a central bank in the United States controlled by the international bankers from London.

The banking privilege, which had been sought after for so long, was now finally in the hands of the globalists. The seizure of the money making privilege, and the control of credit by the bank, guaranteed the necessary power to establish the funding instrument for an inevitable Global World Government. The ability to expand and contract credit was securely in the hands of the internationalists. Now they had the ability to centralize and concentrate capital into the hands of an elite group that could control the world.

Over the last ninety some years, the sinister brilliance of the Fed has looted the American people and created enormous national debt. The ability for it to create fiat money (money not backed by silver or gold) by simply making a notation in a ledger created great inflationary forces and led to the creation of the graduated income tax.

The internationalists also have controlling interests in munitions companies and reap huge profits from war. Governments must buy from them to fight the wars that the internationalists create. The borrowing nations must then promise to pay back the capital needed for their war machines by issuing promissory notes called bonds. The greatest borrower of these funds is America. The combined debt of the world does not equal the amount of borrowed capital that America owes in issued bonds.

The government can make these pledges (bonds) of repayment to the Fed because the people of the United States yearly pay their taxes (graduated taxes) which guarantee repayment. These massive yearly revenues have come under the control of the Fed.

THE CONQUEST OF AMERICA

When America finally lost control of her money, she gave up financial freedom. It can be said that when America lost control of her money she was ostensibly recaptured by Britain—or, more specifically, by those who control Britain.

Very slowly, almost without perception, America has become and is becoming a socialized nation. The manipulation of our monetary system by the creation of debt and the necessity for high taxes is creating a situation where more and more freedom is being lost. This phenomenon is eliminating the middle class and creating a neo-feudalism. The average American doesn't realize he has become captured and enslaved by taxation by the very dragon his forefathers escaped from some two hundred years ago. The Bible says, "Who is able to make war with [the beast]?" (Revelation 13:4).

America began as a nation with a recognition of God and the Bible as a powerful influence on its foundation, the United States Constitution. The erosion of that foundation and the seizure of this once great and free nation has taken place gradually without the detection and knowledge of the populace.

CHAPTER TWENTY-ONE

History of the False Prophet—
Anglo-Americanism

A Global World Government in the modern era should not be viewed as a nineteenth century idea. The powerful forces of the Illuminati that unleashed the French Revolution in 1789 clearly show that a New World Global Order has been in the making since the eighteenth century.[1]

Throughout the 1800s in the United States the idea of globalism was maintained by forces within the British Empire. Three prominent men in the latter part of the century who kept the dream moving forward were John Ruskin, Cecil Rhodes, and Alfred Milner. Their desire was to unite the English speaking people of the world, and to create a global commonwealth of nations patterned after the ideals of the British Empire, but controlled by English speaking people of the aristocracy for the good of the world.[2]

RUSKIN, RHODES, AND MILNER
The Round Table

John Ruskin, mentor of both Cecil Rhodes and Alfred Milner (father of the Round Table), was an ardent student of Plato's *Republic*, the same well from which Karl Marx drank.

Ruskin believed that the state should take control of the means of all production and distribution and organize them for the good of the people. "My continual aim has been to show the eternal superiority of some men to others, sometimes even of one man to all others." Ruskin taught that the ruling class of England had a world mission.[3]

The World Mission

Ruskin taught the students of Oxford University that they were the next leaders of the mission. They were the ones who would carry on the tradition, the possessors of a magnificent tradition of education, rule of law, beauty, freedom, decency, and self-discipline. He taught them that this tradition could not be saved unless it was extended to the lower classes of England and to the non-English masses of the world. If these two classes were not reached, the upper-class Englishmen would ultimately be submerged by these majorities, and the tradition would be lost.[4]

Cecil Rhodes

Cecil Rhodes was one student in attendance those days, and he caught the vision. As a result, with support from Lord Rothschild, he launched a lifetime of concerted efforts to federate the world.[5] His ambitious goals included:

1. The extension of the British rule throughout the world;
2. Perfecting a plan of emigration from the United Kingdom for colonization by British subjects of all lands where the means of livelihood are attainable by energy, labor, and enterprise;
3. *The ultimate recovery of the United States of America as an integral part of the British Empire;*

4. The consolidation of the whole Empire;
5. A system of colonial representation in the Imperial Parliament which may tend to weld together the disjointed members of the Empire;
6. *The foundation of so great a power* as to hereafter render wars impossible and promote the best interests of humanity.

All this he endeavored to do without mention of material reward, an idea fashioned after the religious brotherhood of the Jesuits, "a church for the extension of the British Empire."[6]

The ideas of these men, advanced by the backing of Anglo-American banking houses, created secret societies, which in turn made secret agreements between England and the United States. These secret treaties brought the two countries together into an Anglo-American alliance with the secret goal of a New World Global Order. In England the secret society, which operated in London, was called the Round Table.[7]

THE LEAGUE OF NATIONS

When the planned seizure of the United States economy finally occurred in 1913, the formation of the two-horned beast (the world capital conglomerate) was complete. The conquest of mammon (money) enabled the concentration of financial power in the hands of an elite. What they needed now was a new world political system to manage the aspirations of the British dreamers.

The first attempt at a New World Order was the League of Nations. It came at the culmination of World War I. The general idea of the League of Nations started during the war with a group of Allied statesmen, notably British and American.[8] Winston Churchill supports this view.

The League of Nations was an Anglo-Saxon conception arising from the moral earnestness of persons of similar temperament on both sides of the Atlantic.[9]

THE LEAGUE FAILS

The League of Nations, which was put forward by Woodrow Wilson, failed to gain entire acceptance. Paradoxically, though the rest of the world accepted the idea of the League of Nations, factions within the United States resisted the plan. The plan to create a League of Nations failed.

THE COUNCIL ON FOREIGN RELATIONS

Other powerful men who were disciples of Ruskin joined their lives and fortunes with Rhodes and later formed the Round Table. Alfred Milner became the chief trustee after Rhodes' death. Round Table groups were established in other protectorates and the United States. In 1919-27 the U.S. group became known as the Council on Foreign Relations, or the CFR.[10]

The story of how the secret society of Rhodes/Milner axis extended its influence to the United States is supplied by Dr. Carroll Quigley:

> The American branch of this organization, called at times the Eastern Establishment, has played a very significant role in the history of the United States. Since 1925 there have been substantial contributions from wealthy individuals and from foundations, and firms associated with the International Banking Fraternity, especially the Carnegie United Kingdom Trust, and other organizations associated with J.P. Morgan, the Rockefeller and Whitney families, and the associates of Lazard Brothers and of Morgan, Granfell, and Company.[11]

The CFR today has over two thousand members who represent the elite in government, labor, business, finance, communications and the academy. The primary reason the CFR remains virtually unknown to the American people is because of Article II of the CFR bylaws. This article requires that the meetings of the membership remain secret, and anyone releasing the contents of these meetings is subject to instant dismissal.[12]

The Motivation for the CFR

The intellectuals who founded the CFR felt there was a need for a world government but that the American people were not ready for it. After the League of Nations treaty failed to pass the Senate, the CFR was founded specifically to condition the people to accept a world government as being a desirable solution to the world's problems.[13]

Many of the founders had been involved in the negotiations leading to the Treaty of Versailles after World War I, including: Colonel Edward House (who was secretly involved in the selection of Woodrow Wilson and operated behind the scenes as a secret secretary of state); Walter Lippmann (later to become one of the liberal establishment's favorite syndicated columnists); John Foster Dulles (later to become President Eisenhower's secretary of state); Allen Dulles (later to become the director of the Central Intelligence Agency); and Christian Herter (later to become Dulles' successor as secretary of state).[14]

Financiers of the CFR

The original money behind the CFR came from J.P. Morgan, John D. Rockefeller, Bernard Baruch, Paul Warburg, Otto Kahn, and Jacob Schift, among others. Two of those named above were present at Jekyll Island for the drafting of the Federal Reserve Act. Two of the most outstanding names were J.P. Morgan and Paul Warburg, who (through Kuen Loeb and Co.) represented the Rothschilds of England.[15]

On November 25, 1959, in an issue of its own publication, *Foreign Affairs*, Study No. 7, the CFR detailed its own exact purpose:

> Advocating the building of a new international order
> which may be responsible to world aspirations for
> peace, and for social and economic change; an interna-
> tional order including states labeling themselves as
> socialist (Communist).

The words "new international order" are catch words for a New World Global Government.[16]

The Testimony of an Insider

This is what former Rear Admiral Chester Ward (U.S. Navy, ret.), who was a member of the CFR, told the American people about the intention of the CFR.

> The power clique in these elitist groups have one objective in common; they want to bring about the surrender of the sovereignty and the national independence of the United States.
>
> A second clique of international members in the CFR comprise the Wall Street International Bankers, and their key agents. They want the world banking monopoly from whatever power ends up in control of global government. They would probably prefer that this be an all powerful United Nations Organization, but they are also prepared to deal with a One World Government controlled by the Soviet Communists if the U.S. sovereignty is ever surrendered to them.[17]

Ward went on to say that their overall influence is used in promoting disarmament, subverting U.S. Sovereignty, and suppressing national independence into an all-powerful One World Government.

Membership in the CFR reads like a veritable "who's who" in American politics. Forty-seven members of the American delegation to the founding of the UN were CFR members. At least twelve of the last eighteen secretaries of the treasury were CFR members. At least twelve of the last sixteen secretaries of state have been CFR members. The Department of Defense, created in 1947, has had fifteen secretaries, nine of which have been CFR members. Every Allied commander in Europe and every U.S. ambassador to NATO has been a member of the CFR.[18] Since the inception of the CFR, almost every U.S. president has been a member. Although Ronald Reagan was not, his key appointees were.[19]

The CFR and the Round Table form the hidden governments of the United States and Great Britain. They have been forged together for the purpose of bringing about the dream of Ruskin and Rhodes: a New World Global Order.[20]

CHAPTER TWENTY-TWO

The Two-horned Beast

I t should be no secret at this point that the two horns of the second Beast are the two alleged Christian nations *Great Britain and the United States of America.*

These two nations—through secret Anglo-American agreements that began in the late 1800s—were brought together and are moving the whole world into a Global World Government, or New World Order.[1] It is the function of the two-horned Beast to serve the interests of the Beast system. "And he…causeth the earth and them which dwell therein to worship the first beast" (Revelation 13:12). Here is the clear scriptural evidence that this second Beast, the False Prophet, works to construct the last phase of the first Beast.

These two horns, or kingdoms, were taken over by the international money powers seated in London. The world community views both the United States and England as Christian nations, but the truth is that underneath the appearance there is a *hidden government.* "He had two horns like a lamb, and he spake as a dragon" (Revelation 13:11).

The inability to see this as fulfillment of biblical prophecy is due to the lack of a clear perception of European and American history. In addition, we get no help from Western theologians that remain in darkness, blinded by the dualism of their dispensational theology and a naiveté that arises from a "Yankee Doodle" gospel. It is a sad fact that America has become an instrument of unrighteousness in the hands of the god of this world. The failure to perceive this truth perpetuates the descent into darkness.

The Bankers' Money Machine

Wars and Rumors of Wars

It is through the creation of "wars and rumours of wars" (Matthew 24:6) that the internationalists have been able to create the condition that warrants a global socialistic state. They have flooded the world with red ink and have brought economic bondage through debt and usury, thereby enslaving the people of the world. How do wars and rumors of wars create debt and usury?

When the Federal Reserve Bank was created in 1913, it effectively mobilized the credit of the United States of America. This meant that the Fed, along with the European banking system, had the necessary resources to lend to the nations on new and unprecedented levels. Now, with this new tool in hand (the labor force of the United States guaranteeing loans to the world), the internationalists could swamp the world in debt.

How? By creating wars so that nations must borrow to build their war machinery. It takes billions to build great warships, planes, and weapons for warfare. Imagine the bank that would underwrite loans to the nations energized for war. This is exactly the motivation that empowered the global planners: the creation of war just to make tremendous sums off interest from loans to the nations. One could even back both sides since the outcome made no difference and interest income would be made from both sides. Then, after the war ended, nations would have to rebuild their infrastructure; loans would be made to rebuild the houses, the factories, the businesses. Over time, this moneymaking strategy could produce absolute economic power over the entire earth.

It is an interesting coincidence that World War I began in 1914, immediately after the internationalists established control of the American banking system (the Federal Reserve) and the mobilization of American credit. The beginning of the hostilities that plunged the whole world into war are unclear to this day. Could it have been the international bankers that started the war to end all wars?

Through intrigue, through stealth, through manipulation of the nations, this has been the plan of the international banker elite: seizure of the earth through the creation of enormous debt. The magnitude of the global debt is staggering. The United States has been completely seized and enslaved. The national debt of the United States is greater than the total debt of the entire world.[2]

THE COLD WAR

In the Western world (especially North America) the apparent collapse of communism in Eastern Europe has been lauded as democracy's greatest triumph, a tribute to the success of the free enterprise system. What has not been perceived, however, is that communism has produced the first stages of a global socialism. It has come about by communism serving as a counterweight to capitalism. The cold war between the East and West created huge military expenditures for both sides to maintain the balance of power. The need for both parties to maintain military equilibrium created the necessity for enormous amounts of capital.

The bankers stood ready to loan. Once again, the use of the bankers' insidious printing press—and their ability to foment wars and rumors of wars—has further mired the world in debt. Thus, the bankers greatly advanced their economic grasp and control of the planet.

Since communism has been a chief ingredient for the bankers scheme in this decade, let's back up and trace its roots.

COMMUNISM

The notion of communism as British invention is not a new idea. The articulation of communism was put forward by Karl Marx, whose mentor was British industrialist Frederick Engels. The primary reason for the expounding of this politico-economic ideology was to thwart the spread of democracy to Europe, which was advancing and succeeding in the United States. The foundational principles of nation building expressed in the Monroe Doctrine, based upon George Washington's advice of avoiding entanglements with Europe, had to be countered. These principles were beginning to be imported into Germany, and they posed a tremendous threat to British economic supremacy. The Industrial Revolution that came to the British Isles brought astounding revenues into the coffers of the Bank of England and the Empire itself.[3]

The controllers of Britain were fearful of potential competition on the world scene. They didn't want the rest of the world to industrialize and compete with British goods and markets. Thus came the *Communist Manifesto* and *Das Capital,* whose fundamentals at the time espoused international free trade which, of course, was a contradiction to the Monroe Doctrine's ideology of protectionism.

Internationalism was a tremendous advantage for the British since they already had control of world markets, and it was a terrible disadvantage to the rest of the world, whose economies were already exploited by the British.

Communism was invented by British subjects, but its basic elements were taken from Illuminism. The basic strategy of communism was *to stage economic war* with continental Europe and the United States. The objective was to rule the maintenance and control of world markets. The actual roots of communism go back to Adam Weishaupt.[4]

THE NEW WORLD ORDER IN THE TWENTIETH CENTURY

Later in the twentieth century, when the idea of globalism had matured, the front for the breakout of the New Global World Order was exported to Russia in the Bolshevik Revolution.[5] The czar would not borrow from the Western banks, which would have enslaved Russia through debt and usury. He had to be overthrown.

The ideology of world communism (having been established through the internationalist-financed Bolshevik Revolution of 1917) established the necessary counterbalance: communism weighted against democracy/capitalism. Since World War II, the two have melded into an emerging global socialistic state.

The initial funding for the revolution came from a Rothschild-controlled banking house in the United States called Kuen Loeb and Co.[6] The leadership and intelligence of the movement was supplied by various Marxists who lived in New York. Some were Jews who had become atheists and repudiated their ancient Hebraic ancestry. Many were not Jews, but all, like Karl Marx, had a fanatical political zeal to build a nation state that would encompass the whole world, a global Masonry. Although the primitive breakout of this ideology can be traced to the French Revolution in 1789, the Bolshevik Revolution further advanced what is yet to come: a "World Government to be seated in Jerusalem."[7]

After the Revolution, the Russian state struggled to keep on its feet, and had it not been for the propping up of the Russian economy by the West, there would have been total failure of that regime during the '20s and '30s.

When WWII was coming to an end, the Allies allowed the war to drag on unnecessarily, thus giving an opportunity to the Russians to seize Eastern Europe. A window of truth that supports this allegation can be seen in General Patton's march through Italy, which was mysteriously rerouted through France. Why was he not allowed to invade Germany and end the war? He was willing, ready, and able to take his troops into Berlin.

This military faux pas has never been understood by the world, but the truth is that the Russians needed time to come down into Eastern Europe. The bankers needed their antithesis. The politicians followed orders. General Patton was too good at being a soldier and military man; he was messing up the predetermined plan of the plotting bankers.

These strategic political decisions were made to enable communism to serve as the great antithesis to capitalism. This would lead the way for the inevitable synthesis of capitalism and communism into global socialism, which has now begun to emerge worldwide.

The successful effect of the antithesis (USSR) upon the West, when one lives in the West, is difficult to discern. The international megacorporations owned by the international elite have created the tyranny of centralized capital, and the increasing disappearance of the American entrepreneur. Freedom is being lost quickly, and the ability to compete against the enormity of centralized capital is almost impossible. The tremendous debt created by the necessary military defense of America from the antithesis (Russia) has enslaved the West.

THE COMING TROUBLE

In the Middle East another plot was unfolding, and the bankers fingerprints were all over it. Earlier in the century the British Round Table, under the leadership of Lord Balfour, determined to make the land of Palestine a Jewish homeland. Principally involved in this decision making was the Rothschilds, the principal owners of the Bank of England. The British mandate came to be know as the Balfour Declaration, but the Jewish banking house of Rothschild was in the middle of the mix. Even though the Rothschilds had abandoned their biblical Judaism, they maintain—as do all Jews—a genetical patriotic sense of loyalty to the land of the patriarchs. After the homeland for the Jews was set up in 1917, the Rothschilds were involved in extensive purchases, literally buying back the land from the Arabs. Today, the land contains five million Jews, thanks to the political and economic efforts of the Rothschild. But is this current return of the Jews that which the ancient prophets long ago predicted?

While it took the Balfour Declaration, two world wars, and the Holocaust to set up the state of Israel, it is not the fulfillment of biblical prophecy as most Christians believe. The shocking fact of the matter is that, through extensive writings by contemporary Christian writers, Christians falsely have been led to believe that this is the case. *But it is clear that the theocratic state of Israel will not be set up by man—not even the contrivances of powerful and deceitful bankers of Jewish origin.*

> And it shall come to pass in that day, that the Lord shall set his hand again the second time to recover the remnant of his people...and shall assemble the outcasts of Israel, and gather together the dispersed of Judah from the four corners of the earth.
>
> *Isaiah 11:11,12*

This particular scripture is often cited by Christians as the fulfillment of prophecies for the Jews' current return to Zion. But under close scrutiny, this promised second return of the Jews to the land will occur during the millennial kingdom.

Scripture, if read in context, shows:

> The wolf also shall dwell with the lamb, and the leopard shall lie down with the kid; and the calf and the young lion and fatling together; and a little child shall lead them. And the cow and the bear shall feed; their young ones shall lie down together: and the lion shall eat straw like the ox. And the sucking child shall put his hand on the hole of the asp, and the weaned child shall put his hand on the cockatrice's den.
>
> *Isaiah 11:6-8*

THE REAL NEW AGE

The time period in which this peculiar occurrence takes place has not yet come. These curious traits of animal behavior are unique and have *never* occurred. Nevertheless, they distinctively bookmark the exact nature of that time of return. The time period comes when the whole world is *renewed by God* during the millennial reign of Jesus Christ on earth.

It is during the millennial reign that the curse upon the earth is lifted and these interesting changes in the animal kingdom occur. When that day comes, *then* God will signal for a worldwide return of the Jews to Israel. They will all come home—all, not just a portion. They will live in safety. This is hardly the case today, as Jews live in constant fear of their Muslim neighbors.

Since, according to biblical prophecy, the return of the Jews is yet in the future, then what has the world been witnessing from the beginning of the twentieth century (in the Zionist movement, the Balfour Declaration, and the birth of the state of Israel in 1948)?

THE GREAT SNARE

The answer to this question is both deep and prophetic. What we are witnessing in the Middle East and Israel today is the set up of *the great snare*. David says, "Let their table become a snare before them: and that which should have been for their welfare, let it become a trap" (Psalm 69:22).

Jesus also explained that this *trap* is one that will come over all the earth.

> And take heed to yourselves, lest at any time your
> hearts be overcharged with surfeiting, and drunken-
> ness, and cares of this life, and so that day come upon
> you unawares. For as a snare shall it come on *all them*
> *that dwell on the face of the whole earth.*
> *Luke 21:34,35 (emphasis added)*

The events that are taking place today are all leading to the fulfillment of Scriptures. *These events are the snare to the Jews and a trap to the whole world.* It is the orchestration of these worldwide events that will lead to the fulfillment of the great "weeks" prophecy in Daniel 9:24-27, which we will investigate in the next chapter. While time and space do not permit a careful scrutiny of the whole of this text, it is important to restate the basics for those that have never taken a hard look at this portion of Scripture.

CHAPTER TWENTY-THREE

Daniel's Seventy Weeks

Seventy weeks are determined upon thy people and upon thy holy city, to finish the transgression, and to make an end of sins, and to make reconciliation for iniquity, and to bring in everlasting righteousness, and to seal up the vision and prophecy, and to anoint the most Holy. Know therefore and understand, that from the going forth of the commandment to restore and to build Jerusalem unto the Messiah the Prince shall be seven weeks, and threescore and two weeks: the street shall be built again, and the wall, even in troublous times. And after threescore and two weeks shall Messiah be cut off, but not for himself: and the people of the prince that shall come shall destroy the city and the sanctuary; and the end thereof shall be with a flood and unto the end of the war desolations are determined.

Daniel 9:24-26

This prophecy is the famous "weeks" prophecy that clearly shows the first advent of the Messiah as being sixty-nine weeks from the going forth of a decree. The sixty-nine weeks means sixty-nine units of seven, or sixty-nine "weeks" of years: Sixty-nine weeks, or sixty-nine sevens, equates to 483 years (69 x 7 = 483).

From the time the king of Persia (King Artaxerxes) issued a decree (445 B.C.), exactly 483 years elapsed until Jesus was crucified, or "cutoff." The crucifixion occurred around A.D. 30.

The prophecy begins, however, with Daniel being told that there will be seventy weeks decreed upon his people. The initial decree dealt with a seventy-week period, and the second decree dealt with a sixty-nine week period encompassed by the initial seventy weeks. Initially seventy weeks of years (7 x 70 = 490) were determined, but according to the rest of the scripture, only 483 years transpired. What happened to the last seven years? Seven years are still to be fulfilled in the future. The sixty-nine weeks of years ended at the crucifixion, and the last seven years of the first decree have not yet happened. The suspension of the fulfillment of the prophesy was necessary for the ingathering of the Gentiles. Now, with Jews being gathered back to the homeland in Israel for judgment, history is poised for the last seven years of the prophecy.

> And he shall confirm the covenant with many for one week: and in the midst of the week he shall cause the sacrifice and the oblation to cease, and for the overspreading of abominations he shall make it desolate, even until the consummation, and that determined shall be poured upon the desolate.
>
> *Daniel 9:27*

Here, in verse 27, are the last seven years. The "he" that is referred to is not Jesus Christ, but rather the "prince of the people" that destroys the city of Jerusalem. This prince arrives on the scene to make a covenant with the many during the last seven years, that is, the last week of the seventy weeks. This scripture sums up the advent for the timing of the Antichrist. The Antichrist will come at the beginning of the last seven years of Daniel's seventieth week. He will enforce a deal (no doubt a peace plan) or a covenant with the many for seven years.

All the political manipulations and maneuvering that we are witnessing today is the set up for this world dictator. It is the *trap* on the world that Christ Himself predicted in Luke 21:34,35. It was also foretold by King David of the Jews. We are rapidly approaching the time when a man will step forth and enforce a covenant with the many.

This is before us now in the peace talks and countless attempts for peace in the Middle East. Except for the Islamic states, the people of the world truly hate war. But the peace plans and talks are nothing more than the precursor for *the great snare.* Any guarantee for the enforcement of the peace in the Middle East must be watched as the coming "covenant with the many" spoken of in Daniel. Since the world is near economic collapse due to tremendous worldwide indebtedness, it is possible that the covenant with the many could include an economic agreement.

Since the "weeks" prophecy is to last for 490 years, there will be a seven-year conclusion to purge the Jews, God's people, and to prepare them for the true theocratic state of Israel: the millennium of Messiah.

Though this seven-year period is called a "snare" and a "trap," it will be the means to complete the necessary work of faith in the Jews—which will prepare them for what God chose them for originally. Thus, the nation of Israel has been gathered for judgment, and *not* for a blessing. The present distress is only the beginning.

The orchestration of events that has brought about a return of this remnant has been by the hands of those who have seized control of the reins of international capital. Through political intrigue and the force and power of mammon (the riches of the world), they have seated the Jews in their homeland. God allowed this to take place.

The nation of Israel, as well as the whole world, will be deceived by this prince (Antichrist) who will come during this last week (seven years) of Daniel's prophecy.

God has allowed this to happen with capital controlled by the international world bankers, constructing a global totalitarian socialistic state. The city of Jerusalem eventually will be the seat of the World Government. *The United States' seized economy and the British banking system are the focal points of the war chest for this behemoth undertaking.*

Now, as we enter the final hours before the Antichrist comes, the European economic system (buttressed by the Euro) seems to be strengthening—albeit loosely. How this fulfills Scripture remains to be seen. The face off between the banks of the European continent and the British and American banks double entente is an interesting joust for the moment. The little horn (which grows larger than its associates) has the power to pull three of the ten horns from their roots. Perhaps it will be three kings or nations that refuse to cooperate with the final world banking system. This remains to be seen.

The two horns of the United States and England have effectively and methodically followed the blueprint orchestrating the world into a New Global World Order. Little by little, the construction of the global edifice arises from the sea. The plan of the internationalists is to have their representative seated on the throne of world government when world conditions allow. All diligence is being applied to this end.

The False Prophet, with all the authority of the Beast, uses three methods of power and control for bringing the world into this New Global World Order. The next section deals with each of these methods. They are the tools of the agent of the Antichrist: the False Prophet.

CHAPTER TWENTY-FOUR

Fire from Heaven

And he doeth great wonders, so that he maketh fire come
down from heaven on the earth in the sight of men.

Revelation 13:13

ORVILLE AND WILBUR

When nine- and twelve-year-old Orville and Wilbur
went out to play, little did they realize that their
playful discoveries would revolutionize the world
and drastically alter the way men think about time and space.

Orville and Wilbur Wright stumbled onto the hidden mysteries of flight. Dreams that men had dreamed for thousands of
years were realized by the discoveries of these two unusual boys.
The hidden wisdom of flight was revealed to the inquiring
minds of the two brothers. The mastery of the heavens, which
belongs to the birds alone, was now to be given to man.

In those days provincial minds reasoned, "If the heavens belong to the Lord, then man has no business in the sky. After all, if God had intended man to fly, He would have given him wings like a bird." Today, as we look back on that line of reasoning, we might laugh, but the horrific applications that came as result of the Wright brothers discoveries make us wonder if those old-timers didn't have a point to be made.

If man's incredible intelligence were to be taken away, how could it be said that he is made in the image of God? The real issue, then, is not so much what is known about the principles of the universe but, rather, what is done with that knowledge. This is a matter of conscience.

The problem, of course, is that, collectively, man's record on his trek across the annals of time is very poor when it comes to the use of knowledge. Although in the last one hundred years the world has dramatically progressed technologically, there has been a corresponding decline in morality.

Has technology created a better human race? Morally, the answer is no. Man has become more sophisticated, but his nature remains the same. But this is not an indictment on technology. The peculiar nature of the human race seems to be that man seems to inevitably turn into evil that which is meant for good. Unless man has a remarkable conscience alteration, we all tread on a slippery slope.

THE KNOWLEDGE OF FLIGHT

When the knowledge of flight arrived around the turn of the nineteenth century, it was not considered by the masses to be of any great significance. People did not really believe much would come from it. Yet, within a few short years flight began to play an extremely important role in the First World War. Man had invaded the realm of birds, and now new possibilities lay before him. He had risen above the terrestrial environment and placed himself in the seat of the heavens. Flight!

It had taken thousands of years to arrive, but the unconquerable had been conquered. What was next, the moon? People scoffed. Flimsy little airplanes (Jennies) that were made of balsa wood and cloth could hardly be taken seriously. But eventually more and more was learned. Soon airplanes were able to cross the Atlantic Ocean. A voyage that took months by boat could now be made in a day. The world was made smaller by one man full of courage and bravery.

The momentous transatlantic flight by Charles Lindbergh immortalized flight and made it the most exciting scientific breakthrough of its day. Both Europe and America were startled by the significance of this marvelous and heroic deed. Lindbergh was swamped by crowds and parades as the world marveled at the magnitude of the accomplishment.

The skies today are traversed with ease, as powerful jets move millions of people around the earth yearly. Today, decades later, Lindbergh's flight seems so small, but it was that flight that made a quantum leap in men's minds about the possibilities of flight. One of those possibilities was the utilization of flight for war.

"Nation Will Rise Against Nation"

The imposing of one nation's will over another took on tempting new possibilities with this new technology. The vision of a Global Empire came under consideration in the mind of Adolf Hitler. Soon airplanes were armed with bombs. The world was at war. The airplane that was once made of cloth and balsa was now made of light weight metals and able to lift huge cargoes of weapons.

London and Poland were bombed by Hitler's *Luftwaffe* in his blitzkrieg warfare. In return Germany was bombed by an armada of B17s. Cities were literally incinerated by fire storms. Tens of thousands of people died—not by the explosions of the bombs, but by the intense fire that sucked up all the breathable air.

America discovered how to make nuclear weapons. During the war with Japan in the Pacific, nuclear bombs were dropped on Hiroshima and Nagasaki. The intense fires from the blasts created temperatures as great as those of our sun. The cities were totally destroyed, incinerated by fire. People were burned beyond recognition. Many of those who survived still carry the awful scars in their memories and on their bodies from the fire that came down.

Vietnam experienced the finest technological advancement in fire storms. Massive air raids brought down unimaginable devastation on the country's villages and forests. Napalm bombs wiped out mile after mile and village after village.

More recently, in the Gulf War with Iraq in the early '90s, the awesome air supremacy of the Western nations wrought great fear in the nations of the world. What an object lesson was served to the peoples of the earth. Who would dare go to war with the world's ultimate police force? Fire would come down.

Especially now, many years from that conflict, enormous and incomprehensible strides have been made with laser-guided bombs and rockets. What fear! But the ultimate has yet to come, in the seizures of the utmost high ground.

THE ULTIMATE HIGH GROUND

While military strategists rethink the necessity of airplanes (due to the tremendous success of guided missile technology during Desert Storm), others have revised their thinking concerning Star Wars, or the Strategic Defense Initiative. While uncertainty reigns over the development of this technology most probably it has been *black boxed* and is being secretly funded.

The Star Wars technology is laser technology, the brain child of the Reagan administration. It is the absolute safest defense against incoming missile weaponry.

When it is finished the reality of it being turned over to the United Nations may be unlikely, but whoever controls that system will militarily control the world, for he will have the finest technological ability to call "fire down from heaven."

Finally, there is the UFO phenomena. While this subject lies beyond the credible grasp of the sensibilities of the average person, recently hundreds of testimonies from very credible men suggest that something is up.

One of the more perplexing stories that throws credence into the realm of potentially prophetic fulfillment occurred several years ago. According to high ranking military personnel, an American spacecraft that was headed toward the moon with a nuclear device was disabled by several beams of light from a UFO. It was destroyed, unable to finish its mission. The military believed it to be a plasma beam that disabled the space craft.

These men also testified that the United States has recovered crashed UFOs, and have been able, through their research, to implement technology recovered from the alien spacecraft. Considering the track record of the human race and the nature of man, this is not good news.

> And he doeth great wonders, so that he maketh fire come down from heaven on the earth in the sight of men.
>
> *Revelation 13:13*

CHAPTER TWENTY-FIVE

The Image of the Beast

The agent of Antichrist is, of course, the second Beast of Revelation 13. Who he is has already been revealed. He is dubbed the agent of Antichrist because he is the one who fleshes out a kingdom for the Antichrist at the end of the age.

The kingdom of the Antichrist is a Global World Government the Bible calls the Beast. It was shown in the previous chapter what the ultimate policing power is for this dark utopia, but to control the world there must also be a vast communication system and mind control network. Everyone must be programmed and march to the same drum beat. There must be a universal focal point. There must also be a universal economic system, as shall be pointed out in the next chapter.

What is to be disclosed in this chapter is the second tool or miraculous sign that the False Prophet uses to deceive the nations of the world into accepting the Global World Government.

> And [he] deceiveth them that dwell on the earth by the
> means of those miracles which he had power to do in
> the sight of the beast; saying to them that dwell on the
> earth, that they should make an image to the beast,
> which had the wound by a sword, and did live. And he
> had power to give life unto the image of the beast, that
> the image of the beast should both speak, and cause
> that as many as would not worship the image of the
> beast should be killed.
>
> *Revelation 13:14,15*

In Revelation 13:14, the "image of the Beast" contextually comes into the picture after the healing of a fatal wound to one of the imperial heads of the Beast. Since the various heads of John's first Beast (seven heads in number) have been assigned (Egypt, Assyria, Babylon, Persia, Greece, Rome, and the British Empire), the revived head will be that which comes out of the seven, or seventh.

> And the beast that was, and is not, even he is the
> eighth, and is of the seven, and goeth into perdition.
>
> *Revelation 17:11*

The emergence of the eighth head is clearly the United Nations. It was established out of the fallen (slain) British Empire, empowered by the funding and support of America and domiciled in New York City on Manhattan Island. Its initial inception was sourced in the League of Nations, which failed. President Wilson's League of Nations, with its fourteen points, was the invention of the British Round Table—which in the second decade of the twentieth century sought to establish the Ruskin Rhodes Milner dream. When the League failed, it was renamed the United Nations and set up following World War II. At its core we find British fingerprints, but it was the combined effort of England and the United States that set it up.

The image of the Beast, according to Scripture, occurs after the healing of the fatal head wound to the Beast and the resurrection of the Beast's seventh head into and eighth head. In light of Scripture and history, it is possible that the image of the Beast could have been present in the later part of the 1940s, at the termination of World War II. It is the function of the False Prophet to set up the image of the Beast. Since the False Prophet has been identified as England and the United States (represented by the two horns), the fact that the entity is present in the 1940s assumes that his signs or powers were too.

What Is the Image?

The Greek word that is used to explain the second attesting miracle of powers of the False Prophet is not the word *idol* but the word *eikon*.[1] In the ancient world, an idol was usually a figure that was hand-crafted out of wood or metal. Often it was made in the likeness of an animal or bird. The idol of Molock, for example, had the head of a bull and the hands of a man. Many times, idols were replications of demonic powers, and people would actually bow down and worship them.

Even the ancient Jews fell into this problem and were chastised by God when Aaron made a golden calf that the people bowed down to worship. When Moses, who had gone up to Mt. Sinai to receive the Ten Commandments, came back down, he ran smack dab into this revelry and went ballistic. As a result, God smote the people with a curse and thousands died.

But that is not the word that is used to explain the image of the Beast. The word that explains the image is the word *eikon*. Whereas as an idol is more a vis-a-vis representation of an image, *eikon* is better rendered "likeness." Here is an analogy that helps our understanding. The disciples came to Jesus and asked, "Should we pay taxes?" Jesus answered, "Give me a coin. Whose *eikon* [image] is that?" They said, "Caesar's." The point is that the coin was not an exact replication of Caesar—which is what an idol would be—but rather a likeness of Caesar's image (*eikon*) on a coin.

The False prophet makes an eikon, *a likeness of the Beast, not an exact representation of the Beast.* It is important to remember at this point that the Beast John saw in symbolic form represented *a system of successive empires* stretching from the Egyptian Empire through time to the United Nations.

This brings up an important consideration. What would an *eikon* look like that was a likeness of a system—a geo-political system that has existed for five thousand years? This is a most perplexing and mind boggling consideration!

Nonetheless, the warning from the Law:

> Thou shalt have no other gods before me. Thou shalt
> not make unto thee any graven *image [idol]*, or any
> *likeness* of any thing that is in heaven above, or that is
> in the earth beneath, or that is in the water under the
> earth: Thou shalt not bow down thyself to them, nor
> serve them...
>
> *Exodus 20:3-5 (emphasis added)*

In the Law, God instructed his people concerning idols. Perhaps man's lack of attention to this one principle has set him up for the greatest deception the world has ever known.

The global worship of the Antichrist is the False Prophet's objective. But what does the word *worship* mean? The idea of worship in biblical Greek is best understood as an act of submission, as though one were bending his knee and kissing the hand of a king seated on his throne. This is an accurate picture of worship. It means submission, adoration, reverence, or awe.[2]

In order to evoke this kind of worshipful response from the global masses, the False Prophet gives life—and the ability to speak—to the *eikon* (or icon) of the Beast.

There are two words that explain the word *life* in the Greek language. One is the word *zoe*, and the other is the word *pneuma*. The word *zoe* is the word from which zoology comes, and it means "animate life." *Zoe* is life that only God the creator can give. The word that is given to explain the life that the False Prophet gives is the word *pneuma*. This word pertains to spirit life or spiritual life. Spiritual life is given, but not zoological life.[3] Spirit is intelligence.

In addition, it is clear that the **icon** that speaks, which has spiritual life, also appears after the fatal head wound of the first Beast has been healed. It is the second tool in the hand of the False Prophet, a tool he uses to enslave the whole world in a global worship.

Clearly, the last great global empire was the British Empire, which was slain and now has given way to the eighth head: the United Nations. This could only happen with the presence of the second Beast. Scripture teaches that he is contemporary with the first Beast and that his function it is to build the final form of the Antichrist's system. Through his tools, he builds the final facet of the Beast system. Since he must be on the scene, his tools must also be present; he uses the tools to build the New Global World Order.

But how do you give spiritual life to an icon which represents a system (the Beast system) that is over five thousand years old? What is the icon supposed to look like? The answer to this question is crucial because it is *the* tool (or power) the False Prophet uses to bring the whole world into submission and worship.

What is this image of the Beast, the second power of the agent of Antichrist?

TV: THE IMAGE OF THE BEAST

Since World War II, television has reshaped the American psyche. In all areas—entertainment, politics, marketing, education, and the presentation of news—TV has become the pervasive conveyor to our subconscious and presuppositional psychological grid. It has relocated and replaced the marketplace, the soap box, the pulpit, and the family. On-line shopping, using the same technology as TV, has become a respected and accepted form of shopping. In addition, we have on-line banking. Whether we want to face it or not, television has retooled not only American but world thought and has shrunk the world into a global commune.

With the exception of the workplace, TV is the dominant force in American life. We are rapidly being assimilated by television into a global culture. Because of TV, the world has invaded our homes so that a man's home is no longer his castle or his retreat from the world. It is our marketplace, our political forum, our playground, our school, our theater, our recreation, and our link to an escape from reality. It is the vice which reflects and shapes our assumptions and a means of assaulting those assumptions. It cuts through every socioeconomic, geographic, and cultural group. It is the single binding thread of this country, the one experience that touches young and old, rich and poor, learned and illiterate. A country which was too big for homogeneity, filled by people from all over the globe without any set core of values, America never had a unifying bond. Now we do. Now it is possible to answer the question, What do Americans do? They watch TV.

And how much TV do they watch? The average American family watches the television set for an astounding six to eight hours per day.[4] That means the average child is spending more time watching television than he is going to school. In the 1980s there were more than 150 million TV sets that were turned on for an average of seven hours a day. In the early part of this century it is possible, given the continued growth, that we will spend more hours watching TV than the hours given to sleeping.

We already know the average citizen spends one fourth of his waking hours in front of the television.[5] The only activity that takes more of our children's time is sleeping. There is no question that TV holds unparalleled power over America—more than schools, parents, or churches.

George Gurban, dean of the Annenberg School of Communication of the University of Pennsylvania, put it this way:

> In only two decades from 1946 to 1966 of massive existence, television had transformed the political life of the nation, had changed the daily habits of our people, had molded the style of the generation made overnight. TV had made global phenomena out of local happenings; redirected the flow of information and values from traditional channels to centralized networks reaching into every home.[6]

In other words, TV has profoundly affected what we call the process of socialization, the process by which members of a species interact.

By its reach, TV is so pervasive that it can alter the American idiom overnight. Who can ever forget the phrase, "Where's the beef?" when it swept the nation?

TV has altered the eating and sleeping habits of most Americans. It has kept them up later at night, but it has also kept them home. It has broken the traditional patterns of how children learn. Television has altered the shape and speed of our knowledge of the world.

In the 1930s, even as national radio grew, the mass circulation magazines were a centerpiece of American life for learning the news of the world—and for escaping from it. But by the time network TV was just twenty-five years old, the dominant weekly magazines—such as *Life, Corners,* and *Saturday Evening Post*—had all died out. The most widely circulated magazine was *TV Guide.*

The sheer power and reach of television is one reason why we understand so little about it. Its swift conquest of America can be linked in large measure to the fact that TV, as an instrument, reflected one of the populace's most insistent desires: to be left alone. In 1946, there were 7,000 TV sets in America. In 1947, there were 178,000 sets, with an estimated audience of one million.[7] In 1948, Milton Berle began his run on NBC, which helped explode production to 975,000 TV sets. One year later, 3,000,000 sets were made. By late 1949, TV drew 41 percent of the radio audience. This new medium—by accident more than design—was in the hands of relatively few people. And less and less by accident, these few people found themselves relatively free from effective control and accountability. This system had grown and taken shape in large measure because the invention had created new categories of reality, new sources of power that the government could not even contemplate until they were firmly in place. By mid-century, TV had conquered America.[8]

In one sense, we had expected it all along; in another sense, we never knew what hit us.

CHAPTER TWENTY-SIX

Television:
Snow White's Poisoned Apple

Just how close are we to the return of Christ? How can we see the times and know for sure when that event will take place? Jesus himself reminded us that we were to watch and pray. He warned that, with regard to His Second Coming, we were not to fall asleep. Sleep, of course, is characterized by simply being unconscious.

Today, not only is the world unconscious of the impending return of Christ, but so is the church. The world's unconsciousness is best explained by the scripture where people are saying,

> Where is the promise of his coming? for since the
> fathers fell asleep, all things continue as they were from
> the beginning of the creation.
>
> *2 Peter 3:4*

The church, on the other hand, is like the famous story of Snow White. She was offered the poisoned apple, she took a bite, and she fell into a death-like sleep.

It can be said that, in our time, we have no prophet to show us our signs. The enemy has laid siege to the temple. The poison apple that people have bitten into is television, and the poison continues to spread a deadening sleep. Now we have hundreds of channels to watch, and we can order movies brought directly into our homes. Broadband expands the use of the computer to new levels of fixation and new records of wasted time.

THE COMMON PLAGUE OF SMUT

Major networks continue to loosen their standards attempting to regain those who have strayed. But the overall move of the TV industry is the continuous slide into the bottomless pit of debauchery. If the moral slide of television wasn't enough, the avalanche of smut on the Internet is almost incomprehensible. Pornography accounts for more than 80 percent of the downloaded material coming into our homes. With the onslaught of pornography injected into the viewing public, especially teenagers, we are indeed engulfed in perilous times.

THE SERIAL KILLING

In the final hours before his execution, Ted Bundy, the most infamous of all serial murderers, spoke of the influence of pornography in his life and its subsequent effect on his behavior. He attributed his serial killing to the powerful influence of pornography. If his self-analysis is true, then we can expect an enormous wave of violence upon women and children in the very near future.

WHAT IS MORALITY?

Morality is simply the standard that operates on the human conscience to monitor and control thought and behavior. God placed His ten spiritual laws within the human conscience. These laws were clearly defined to the Jews when Moses received them from God on Mount Sinai thirty-five hundred years ago. The ten spiritual laws were known to the Jews as the Ten Commandments.

These laws reflect God's divine nature; because these laws were placed within man, he is a moral agent. In this sense, mankind is created in the image of God.

When man deviates from these laws (that is, when he transgresses them), and does not seek repentance and forgiveness, his conscience darkens, he loses sight of his identity, and he becomes even less than the animals. Animals are amoral. Mankind, the moral agent, becomes immoral.

Since every man is a transgressor of his conscience, he is caught in a trap. His failure to act in the way he knows in his conscience is right creates guilt. The conscience of man monitors good and evil, both externally and internally. That is, it was designed by God to screen thoughts that enter our mind through environmental effects, and it also monitors our personal thoughts that arise from within.

When the conscience is operating in a healthy capacity, it will reject immoral thoughts that are in conflict with the laws of God, which are written on the inner conscience. Thus, morality functions in direct relationship with human conscience. The human conscience, to be perfectly clear, is like the door to a castle: once it is broken down, the castle can be overcome. Pornography is an attack on the moral conscience.

Morality, based on the God-given law inscribed on the human conscience, was verified to the Jews on stone tablets. These laws clearly express God's standard of righteousness and form the basis of human morality. In the Western world, this concept is expressed as the Judeo-Christian ethic.

The human conscience stands to defend the inner person (or the subconscious) from the attack on morality. As human beings grow, they are either reinforced in their conscience, thus defending their inner person, or they are inundated and eroded by the opposite forces, which mitigate against this principle. This was the fate of Bundy, who became the serial killer.

Since the world defines the inner person as the subconscious mind, it is hard to make a point as to what the spiritual implications are in this context. Most people, including

Christians, accept the notion that whatever isn't conscious mind is subconscious mind. They accept the world's definition as true. The fact of the matter is, what men call the subconscious mind is actually a man's spirit. The attack upon morality is an attack on the door to a man's spirit. If the door (conscience) is broken in, the man's inner temple (his spirit) is assailed and— as in Ted Bundy's case—possessed.

Since we are spirit encased in flesh, the attack on our spirit is an attack on who we are. It is an assault on our personal identity. Ted Bundy is a classic example of the war that rages over a man's temple. Bundy became the antithesis of what God intended for him to be.

How the Tool Works

TV has been seized by forces that long ago began, on a massive scale, to break down the foundation of Western Civilization. The Judeo-Christian ethic must, in the eyes of the world planners, be overthrown in order to create a One World Global Government. The stakes are high, as more and more people bite into the forbidden fruit of TV's slide into smut.

To bring this into focus, it must be seen that if there is to be a final hour of organized lawlessness, it must begin with a total breakdown of God-defined morality—so that men might be conformed to a global empire. Since the founding fathers of this great nation developed the Constitution based on a Judeo-Christian ethic, this country remains an obstacle in the plans for a New World Order. If ever one wanted to make a case for a restraining force, America would be a good topic of conversation. Take America out of the world as a Christian nation and watch what happens. But this is exactly what TV and the Internet have done to this country. The Judeo-Christian morality is sinking fast. Destroying Christianity is exactly what the New Global World Order is about.

The New World Order Morality

This empire will not be based on laws of conscience placed there by God.

TV has insinuated itself quickly into the global psychological fabric of man's subconsciousness. It is *the* major tool being used to reshape the world away from the Judeo-Christian ethic and into a new international standard, a standard that is not based on God's original intent for judging thought or behavior. It could be said that the basic spirit of TV, with fewer and fewer exceptions, is Antichrist.

This media assault on the human conscience through the display of sexual immorality requires us to cautiously monitor what is viewed. Our liberty in Christ must not be an occasion for license. We must carefully screen our TV viewing. We must endeavor, with all diligence, to keep our heart pure.

This particular section has dealt with TV and its derivative, computer monitors (which are the same technology). This technology is clearly an instrument in the hands of the global planners.

CHAPTER TWENTY-SEVEN

The Law

When God gave the Law (the Ten Commandments) to the Jews, He was placing before them the mirror of their inner man. Since God's laws are written within every man, the ten Laws given to Moses were merely the reflection of man's conscience. What was the purpose? The Law was given to bring clarification to a man's conscious mind. This explanation of God through Law was both good and bad. It was good in that it declared He was selecting a people for Himself and revealing to them His nature expressed in Law. It was bad, however, in that it laid out a standard that was virtually impossible to live by.

The Law is perfect because it was handed down by a perfect God. But when imposed on people, the Law was unlivable. The Law created a contrast between the perfect morality of a righteous

God and imperfect and fallible man. No matter how hard any man tried, he could never live this Law perfectly. Thus, the Law, expressing the holy and righteous characteristics of God, became a curse. The Jews, who were called to live the Law, found themselves with the incredible dilemma of constantly dealing with the reality of sin—that is, the transgression of the Law.

How could these laws that rule the conscience—having been reinforced by the Ten Commandments on stone tablets— also show man to be a transgressor? The answer is that without a clear understanding of man's true predicament, every man would be schizophrenic. On the one hand the human conscience agrees with the Law given by Moses, but, on the other hand, man cannot perform the Law in his behavior or thought life. Man is both like God, in that his conscience shows the work of the Law, and like the devil, in that he tends to be against the very things he agrees are right and proper in his conscience.

MENTAL DISEASE

What does all this mean? The only solution for this predicament is to concede that man's conscience isn't strong enough by itself to control a man's behavior. This paradox of conscience and a man's natural behavior (that daily functions in contradiction to his conscience) is the very source of most mental disease.

When God gave the Law (Ten Commandments) to the Jews, He actually gave an unlivable standard. Wasn't that cruel? Why did He do that? He did that to clearly point out that man's nature had become estranged from God's self-sacrificing nature verses man's self-centered nature. The Law was given to break through to man and enable him to see his estrangement. God's ways are not nearly the ways of man. God's thoughts are much higher than man's thoughts.

God's purpose was not only to show the contrast between God and man but also to show the impossibility of man ever attaining the likeness of God by the sheer power of obedience to His Law. The Old Testament Law only made man more mindful of his moral inability. The Law as a covenant could never bring man into perfection. We acknowledge this fact when we say a man is "only human."

But how could God accomplish His plan to bring man to the point where he can perfectly obey and live the perfect Law?

The Atonement

When God gave Moses the Law, He knew man could not live up to its lofty standards. He gave the Law to make man mindful of his shortcomings and sinfulness. However, along with the Law, God instituted the Jewish animal sacrificial system as the atonement principle, which makes amends for man's inability to live up to the standard of the Law. Although the animal sacrificial system was rudimentary in teaching man about justice, it was established to show that when a transgression of the Law occurred—either individually or corporately—there had to be a penalty assessed and a price paid for that particular transgression.

If a man committed murder, he was to die himself. If there was adultery, then a punishment for that sin was to be meted out. But, to approach God after a transgression, there also had to be the spilling of the blood of animals. The animal sacrifices required a priesthood to administrate the religious ordeal. The tribe of Levi was selected for this special responsibility. Is God a bloodthirsty God?

It is the holiness of God that requires the satisfaction for the transgression of the Law. Disobedience to the Law was, and is, a depletion from the life of God. In order for man to be in right standing with God, there had to be the remitting of that sin. The expiation of that sin was achieved through blood. "For it is the blood that maketh an atonement for the soul" (Leviticus 17:11).

The Law and animal sacrificial system were instituted only to instruct and thus lead to a better and more perfect contract with God. This is the New Covenant.

The New Covenant

The Law could not bring man's conscience into perfection, nor by man's will could it be lived. Therefore, because the atonement for sin was a yearly ordeal, man he was constantly in remembrance of his transgressions. His conscience was continuously in a state of conflict with his behavior. Since man knows the Law intrinsically, he does not need legal knowledge. Rather, he needs *power* to enable him to live above the motions of disobedience within himself that operate against his conscience. Since the old Law needed the blood of animals to bring about the remission of sin, God sent in His Son Jesus, a more perfect sacrifice. Through His blood, man could finally have a "once and for all" atonement principle. In addition the very life of God Himself, the Holy Spirit was sent to empower man to escape the clutches of sin.

Through proper understanding and response to the New Covenant, mankind can be free from mental disease—since mental disease is merely the result of suppressed guilt. Guilt, of course, is the feeling upon the conscience that occurs when one violates the Law. If proper response to the atonement through Christ's blood is not invoked, then guilt is shoved down through the door of the conscience into the human spirit (subconscious). Mental disease is a legal problem with God that requires a payment against a violation of God's Law. The problem is complicated in that, in God's court, you are guilty when you violate the Law. But when an appeal is made to God on the grounds of the blood of Jesus Christ (the New Covenant), quickly there is an immediate release from guilt.

CHAPTER TWENTY-EIGHT

"Here Is Wisdom"

And that no man might buy or sell, save he that had the
mark, or the name of the beast, or the number of his
name.

Revelation 13:17

Jesus had much to say about money and riches. In fact,
throughout the Scripture, many references speak of the
power and transient nature of the riches of this world. Two
examples are found in Proverbs.

Wilt thou set thine eyes upon that which is not? for
riches certainly make themselves wings; they fly away as
an eagle toward heaven.

Proverbs 23:5

> When thou sittest to eat with a ruler, consider diligently
> what is before thee: And put a knife to thy throat, if
> thou be a man given to appetite.
>
> *Proverbs 23:1,2*

In other words, wealth can buy people. Money has the power to make men compromise values.

THE ANTICHRIST WILL MASTER MONEY

The coming world ruler, the Antichrist, will not only gain mastery over mammon; he also will be the consummate money manager when he ends up with all the gold, silver, costly stones, and treasures.

> But in his estate shall he honour the God of forces: and
> a god whom his fathers knew not shall he honour with
> gold, and silver, and with precious stones, and pleasant
> things.
>
> *Daniel 11:38*

> But he shall have power over the treasures of gold and of
> silver, and over all the precious things of Egypt...
>
> *Daniel 11:43*

When Jesus spoke on wealth he used the phrase "mammon of unrighteousness." The word *mammon* in the ancient world meant "riches," akin to a Hebrew word meaning "to be firm, steadfast"; hence, mammon is that which is trusted.[1]

> No man can serve two masters: for either he will hate
> the one, and love the other; or else he will hold to the
> one, and despise the other. Ye cannot serve God and
> mammon.
>
> *Matthew 6:24*

In other words, one is either serving God or money. He either puts his trust in one or the other.

During the temptations of Christ in the wilderness, the prince of this world, Satan, offered Jesus the kingdoms of the world and all their glory. There was a catch to the offer: Christ had to first bow down and worship him. Jesus passed on the deal, but someone will succumb (or already has succumbed) to that temptation and will take the devil up on it.

When that day finally comes, the means for world control will come through the concentration and accumulation of wealth or mammon. The god of this world is mammon, and he who controls mammon will control the world.

Since 2 Thessalonians 2:1-12 teaches that the coming of the day of the Lord will be preceded by the Antichrist, the forces pressing the world toward the New World Order will be noticed in the place where wealth is accumulating and concentrating. When the final and complete mastery of wealth is accomplished, Antichrist will soon appear, and the failure of mammon will follow.

Scripture instructs the faithful to:

> Make to yourselves friends of the mammon of unrighteousness; that, when ye fail, they may receive you into everlasting habitations.
>
> *Luke 16:9*

When mammon fails, those who put their reliance in it will be enticed into a new economic system.

THE NEW GLOBAL ECONOMIC SYSTEM

The new system, as predicted in Revelation, will no longer have any medium of exchange that man historically has been accustomed to using. What is coming is a total departure from anything man has ever known in the transacting of goods and services. There will be absolutely no exchange currencies such as dollars or coin or gold or silver. It is described in the book of Revelation as a system where only a mark is utilized.

> And he causeth all, both small and great, rich and poor, free and bond, to receive a mark in their right hand, or in their foreheads: And that no man might buy or sell,

save he that had the mark, or the name of the beast, or the number of his name.

Revelation 13:16,17

Human nature is a strange thing. Usually, people do not make changes in their lives unless they are struck by a tragedy or a catastrophe of some sort. Since people naturally resist change, they will especially not favor changes in the way business is transacted today.

It is because of this human characteristic the coming cashless system is gradually being foisted on the peoples of the world. Its coming is hardly being noticed. It is being phased in through electronic funds transfer and debit cards.

In order for its final form to be imposed, however, there will, in all probability, be a great depression or world banking collapse. The United States' debt continues to soar more than six trillion dollars. The population of the United States is 288,182,942. That does not include illegal immigrants. Each citizen's share of that debt amounts to $21,442.07. The debt is not static; it has been growing at the rate of more than a billion dollars per day since September 28, 2001. This incredible debt explosion (along with the J.P. Morgan Chase Manhattan derivatives exposure) places the system ever closer to a massive collapse. When the economic system sputters and fails, the timing will be ripe for a cashless system.

JUSTIFICATION FOR A CASHLESS SYSTEM
The Great Works of Cainism

There are in the world today a great many complicated and distressing problems that a cashless system would seemingly correct, thus making a cashless system seem justifiable and reasonable.

1. Drugs

The international drug cartel could not operate and would fold overnight. A cashless society, run by a mark on the hand or the forehead, would eliminate the world's greatest social problem.

If there were no cash, local and domestic growers would not be able to sell their goods.

Since drug money cannot be taxed, huge fortunes accumulate within the drug cartels, and the money barons (the Fed) cannot regulate it.

The people of the U.S. would do almost anything to stop the flow of drugs, due to their destructive effect on the youth.

The price tag to fight drugs through military expenditures would be cut to almost zero.

2. Counterfeiting

As technology progresses, almost any novice today with the right equipment can counterfeit currency. During WWII, millions and millions of bogus dollars were printed in Eastern Europe. This counterfeit currency flooded the market, causing great damage to our economic system. The destruction of a country's currency is a form of warfare. A mark that would eliminate cash would safeguard against the counterfeit currency problem.

3. Credit Card Fraud

Credit card fraud, which now amounts to tens of billions each year, and the subsequent wrecking of people's credit through stolen cards would be totally eliminated.

4. Illegal Immigration

The uncontrolled influx of illegal immigration, which destabilizes economic systems, would totally stop. Remember, no one can buy or sell without a mark. And those coming into a country instantly would be tracked and found.

5. Underground Economy

In every nation there is an underground economy that goes untaxed. Hundreds of billions of dollars flows through the underground economic system in the U.S. alone. The underground economy in other nations is the dominant system of those countries. How does a nation pay its debts without taxation? And how can a government tax income that cannot be tracked?

Underground economies, typified by merchants selling goods on street corners, are growing in South America, draining billions of dollars in taxes and other revenues from their financially troubled governments.

Even self-employed professionals such as doctors, dentists, lawyers, and psychologists are going underground. The underground network provides millions of jobs—and extra income for the otherwise unemployed, but experts say the gross national product of many countries would grow 50 percent or more if underground economies were counted.

In a recent newsletter distributed in Brazil, the First National Bank of Boston said that the informal economy "dodges direct taxation, but uses public schools and roads. It avoids massive paperwork, government inspection, and the burden of dealing with 38 government entities to make simple business decisions." The bank estimated "an additional 30, 40, or even 50 percent of extra economic activities are out there bubbling away and contributing to a much more sizable gross national product."

6. Crime

A cashless system would eliminate a great deal of crime where the motive was cash. Think of it! All kinds of crime eliminated as money becomes virtually impossible to steal. There would no longer be bank robberies, skimming of funds, diverting of money. Sophisticated white-collar crime would be no more. The economic system would be perfect. The justification for a cashless economy becomes very self-evident when we look at the deteriorating conditions of society.

7. The Federal Debt

If a man gets far over his head in debt, he has to declare bankruptcy. When this happens he has to start over again. After all, you can't get blood from a turnip. The same is true for a country.

The federal debt is so enormous that there is simply no way it can be paid back. Every year the compounding interest and continued borrowing to finance the annual budget deficit worsens the problem. The new monetary system will eliminate the problem. It will streamline the system that simply doesn't work any longer.

The third world nations are already set for any kind of change that will bring them out of their hopelessness—especially nations like Brazil and Argentina and the countries of Africa that are buried under a mountain of debt and cannot meet the interest service, let alone pay off the debt. The United States, in its new spat of deficit spending, is back on the pathway of monumental debt.

8. Health Care

One of the greatest social and political problems of the last several decades is the issue of health care. Although the United States has the greatest health care system in the world, millions of people in the United States are without affordable health care protection. When the taxation problem is solved (through the elimination of the underground economy), the amount of money to finance a universal health care program will immediately materialize. Universal health care will be available for anyone in the world by just taking the mark of the Beast. Imagine that! The mark will establish you as a world citizen.

9. Global Peace

The most appealing aspect of the mark will be a great reduction in the threat of war. Since many wars come from the love of money, eliminate money and eliminate most wars and crimes. The people of the world will see this idea as the greatest boon to peace the world has even known. They will reason that the trade-off, which is the total loss of privacy, they will reason, will be more than worth it. Anyone who doesn't go along with the idea will be viewed as malcontent and rebellious, a war monger, an enemy of the state. How could anyone not want peace? The pressure to conform to the new economic system will be enormous.

The people today who live in the great cities literally fear for their lives. The streets are unsafe. Assaults, rape, and murder are the order of the day and the night. Try wearing the colors of the local street gangs and see what happens. The people of the great cities are ripe for any reasonable answer. The people of earth are weary of conflict and poverty. All that is needed is a round of massive inflation and the new system will flow in on the cries of the people. The new world economic system will make the world safer.

10. Protection from Terrorism

The mark of the Beast will eliminate terrorism. The war on terrorism will ultimately be waged by eliminating cash. The men who destroyed the World Trade Center were able to function because they used cash. If every man woman and child had to be marked with an electronic number, the whole of society could be tracked. This would be an enormous selling point. The world will finally be safe from terrorism.

Y2K SET THE STAGE

After the Y2K bug failed to work its woe, very few people realized the terrible potential for world calamity. More than two hundred billion dollars was spent to correct what could have been history's worst disaster. Those that grasped the terrible danger worked feverishly to rectify the problem. As a result of the colossal effort to fix the problem, the world's electronic interconnectedness was greatly enhanced.

The IRS boasts that before Y2K there were sixteen mainframe computers that managed our entire tax system. Today, as a result of Y2K, there is only one. That is control! All it will take is global fiat currency system failure and the nations will be in position for a total cashless, international, electronic money: the mark of the Beast. The stage is set. All the currencies of the world are fiat. Every currency is being inflated. They are *all* set on a crash course towards worthlessness. It is just a matter of time.

A WORLD BANKING COLLAPSE

Is it really possible that there could be a world banking collapse? Today, all the world's banks are fashioned after the Bank of England. They all fundamentally function the same with what is called "fiat" currency. A fiat currency is a currency that is not backed by gold or silver; they exist by the fiat (or command) of the king. Bankers love fiat currency because contrary to gold which cannot be manipulated, a currency can simply be printed. All you need is ink, paper, and a printing press. In other words it can be inflated. Gold and silver on the other hand must be mined.

An enormous amount of human labor is involved in extracting the precious metals from the earth. Bankers hate gold and silver for this reason. They cannot alter it; they cannot inflate it. It is what it is: real money. Since the beginning of the Clinton administration, the Federal Reserve has inflated the money (cash) supply over 70 percent. Alan Greenspan has created 70 percent more cash flow by simply turning on the printing presses.

As a result, enormous volumes of cash entered the stock market as people took advantage of low interest rates and placed their bets in the stock market. The stock market exploded upward, forming a bubble that in the year 2000 began to burst.

Those who took the exhilarating ride up nervously watched as their paper wealth begin to slowly evaporate. Unfortunately they also took the ride down. The market crashed. But the amazing thing is that the *perception* of the value of the dollar has remained by and large the same. How could this be? The value of gold and silver has been manipulated by the bankers to maintain the *perception* of a stable currency. Gold and silver, even though they no longer are redeemable by currency, still function as a de facto standard of value of a currency. Why? Because precious metals represent real money, or real value.

If the true measure of money can be manipulated, then the perception of inflation on a currency (the bankers' printing press) goes unnoticed. The bankers can continue to print money, which makes currency worth less, but the public never catches on to what is happening to their money.

How do they manage to manipulate the price of gold and silver? Derivatives. They sell derivatives. A derivative is a contract that derives its value from something tangible—in this case, a gold or silver contract. A gold or silver futures contract is paper gold and silver. It is a promise to deliver an order of gold or silver in the future. Let's say Kodak needs a million ounces of silver a year (Kodak uses enormous amounts of silver for film). They want to lock in a price today, but will take delivery in one year. If silver goes up in price, they made a smart decision because they locked in the price and saved money. Had they waited to buy later, it would have cost them more. This is a futures contract. They pay today's price but take delivery in the future.

The advantage for Kodak is they only have to pay a small percentage to control those million ounces of silver until delivery is made a year later. Then they pay the balance. However, the risk is that even if the price of silver goes down, Kodak still has to pay the price the agreed to in the original deal.

These derivatives are used to control the price of the gold and silver commodities. How? By selling enormous amounts of paper gold and silver contracts, they flood the market and drive the price of those commodities down. The paper price effectively drives down the hard gold and silver price. The gold and silver commodities have been rigged and manipulated for years. The big banking houses of J.P. Morgan/Chase, Citibank, Goldman Sacks, and others are involved in concert with the Fed to manipulate the perception of the value of our currency by controlling the price of gold and silver. It is not a free market. But the game is coming to an end.

Their ability to deceive the public is coming to an end. Either the fraud will be exposed or the law of supply and demand will bring the truth out into the light of day. J.P. Morgan/Chase has a twenty-four trillion dollar derivative exposure. They have sold more gold and silver than exists.

What will come is a failure of the money system as we know it. Then the solution will be the mark of the Beast and a cashless system, as predicted in Revelation 13.

CHAPTER TWENTY-NINE

Laser Scanning Systems for Supermarket Automation

> Here is wisdom. Let him that hath understanding count
> the number of the beast: for it is the number of a man;
> and his number is Six hundred threescore and six.
>
> *Revelation 13:18*

When the universal product code (UPC) was invented and introduced in 1973 by IBM (a Rockefeller-owned corporation), there were five variations of the code, classed as A, B, C, D, and E. The A and E versions are most commonly used in grocery applications. Its primary purpose, at the time, was simply daily inventory control. This eliminated the need for grocery stores to go through the tedium of counting what was left on the shelves after each day's business. One could merely take stock by punching in the request to the computer, which calculated the day's business.[1]

Since that time, however, some innovative ideas for new uses of this invention have surfaced, along with some very penetrating insights into just how the bar codes operate.

THE UNIVERSAL PRODUCT CODE

There are three major features of the UPC symbol:

1. The encodation uses varying width intervals of bars and spaces. This eliminates sensitivity to ink spread and allows the symbol to be read by scan lines not perpendicular to the bars.[2]

Fig. 1 UPC symbol showing width intervals for bar codes

2. The symbol can be read as two halves by the laser scanner beam and then combined in the computer system to yield the full 12-digit code.

| Product | Manufacturer |
| ID Number | ID Number |

Fig 2 Two halves of UPC symbol

3. The size of the UPC symbol maybe as large as 200 percent of the normal size, or as small as 80 percent of the normal.

0 16000 66210 4

Guard	Product	Center	Mfr ID	Guard
Bar	ID Number	Bar	Number	Bar

Fig. 3 UPC symbol enlarged to 200 percent

Figures 1,2, and 3 illustrate a standard UPC symbol, which is the machine-readable representation of the UPC code. A standard symbol consists of parallel light and dark bars of varying widths accompanied by numeric characters printed below each data character. The numeric characters are not readable to the computer; it only reads the bar codes. The numeric characters are for human consumption and represent the data which are encoded with the bars.

The left side of the symbol begins with a white margin and the guard bars (see Fig. 3) followed by the encoded number system character. This character is usually identified with a human-readable character immediately outside the left margin. The system character is followed by five characters. These characters represent the number of each particular product. Then in the middle are the center bars, or the center band, which are followed by five more characters representing the manufacturer number. The five data characters are followed by the guard bars and then the white margin.[3]

It is very critical to focus on the understanding that the computer does not recognize numbers as we know them. The computers, with incredible speed, calculate the binary values of 1s and 0s contained in the width of the lines of the bars.

The *data bars* of the UPC carry specific coded information on the product identification information (the left side of UPC) and the manufacturer identification information (the right side of UPC).

The guard bars are, however, different in function than the data bars. The guard bars actually operate the computer. *They are computer programming characters.* They actually tell the computer when to start and stop picking up the data information.[4]

Of vital importance is the binary value of the guard bars. In Figure 4, on the right side of the UPC, the first data character next to the center bar is the data character with the equivalent numeric value of six. If you look at the design of that character, you will see it is exactly the same width as the guard bars.[5]

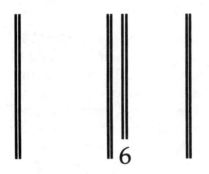

Fig. 4 UPC width design of guard bars

This pattern—light line, space, light line—conforms exactly to the dimensions of the guard bars. Remember, the computer does not know numeric values, only binary values. So, when the electronic scanner goes over the marks on each package as you check out from the grocery store, it is only seeing 1s and 0s. This is also true of the guard bars. The computer is seeing the guard bars in the language of 1s and 0s.[6]

The Numeric Value of the UPC Guard Bars is 666

The most amazing thing is that although the guard bars encoded with three and five modules as 101 and 01010, they operate on the same root as the data character six, which is configured with seven modules. The three bars within the UPC that operate the computer are all (in binary 101 and 01010) or the equivalent of the number of the data character six (see Fig. 5).[7] Though the encodings are different, the visible modules of 101 are the same.

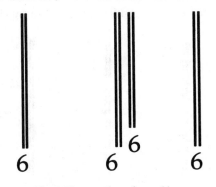

Fig. 5 Binary value of guard bars

The universal product code is a mark run by three sixes. It was designed as a boon to control and keep track of inventory for businesses. When the time is ripe—due to the many global problems and the burgeoning world population—the mark will be applied to everyone for total world monetary control.

> And he causeth all, both small and great, rich and poor, free and bond, to receive a mark in their right hand, or in their foreheads: And that no man might buy or sell, save he that had the mark, or the name of the beast, or the number of his name. Here is wisdom. Let him that hath understanding count the number of the beast: for it is the number of a man; and his number is Six hundred threescore and six.
>
> *Revelation 13:16-18*

THE APPLICATION OF 666

Here is a plausible scenario for how easily this technology can be adapted for a New World Order economic system. Everyone could be given the three programming characters (see Fig. 6).

These characters have been referred to as the guard bars and the center bar of the UPC. Each has a binary value of 101, which equates to the numeric value of six. Ostensibly, each person could be given the three computer programming characters 666.

Fig. 6 The three UPC sixes

Each person could have three sixes which access the computer, and specific information concerning who they are and where they live (see Fig. 7). Then each could be given an electronic banking number.

Fig. 7 Preliminary framework for personal ID number

As can be seen above, the three sixes could serve as the computer programming characters. Then, as shown in Figure 8, the beginning bar codes of data are entered on the left side of the UPC. The data that have been added are 110 and 619.

The number 110 is the corporate ID number of the United States, and 619 is the telephone area code of San Diego. Every nation has a corporate identification number, which indicates the national corporate computer system containing the individual's location (in this example, the United States). The 619 number answers to a local area computer. So we have 61106196. Plausibly, 619 could reference a local computer.

Fig. 8 Data for personal residence

The right side of the UPC could have the PIN (personal identification number). Every child born in the United States is given a Social Security number at birth. The PIN, no doubt, will be linked to that ID number. Since each area code computer system can contain up to 999,999 names, it can be seen that almost one billion names can be stored in the 110 (United States) corporate numbers system. We have added a six digit modified Social Security number that, hypothetically, could answer to the San Diego area computer district.

Once the mark is filled in, we have a completed PIN that allows the individual to do away with all earlier forms of identification. The sixes used to operate the computer by the laser scanner are the universal computer access number.

Fig.9 Completed personal ID number

With this new system, an individual can travel the world without having to carry a passport, driver's license, credit card, or money. No money?

When a purchase is to be made at, say, the supermarket, the laser scanner could simply scan the merchandise. Then, with a handheld scanner, the cashier could scan the customer's hand or forehead (the mark will be on the hand or the forehead) and retrieve the necessary personal information for an electronic funds transfer from that person's electronic banking account. The electronic banking account will be linked directly to the individual's personal information on the right side of the UPC. With incredible speed the EFT (electronic funds transfer) will deduct the amount of the purchase from the individual's electronic account and transfer the funds into the account of the store where the purchase has been made.

EFT technology has now been installed in gasoline stations, restaurants, supermarkets, and every kind of retail agency. Years ago in southern California, a prominent fast food chain initiated the idea using a company called Interlink. The system links certain local banks together in a banking network and allowed a bank card purchase for food at the restaurant. Now this practice is common place. The system automatically deducts the purchase price of the food from the individual's bank account and transfers the funds to the restaurant's bank account. This system has been in place for many years as a forerunner of the coming 666 worldwide cashless system.

BETTER THAN BAR CODES

There are a few limitations with the existing system. The scanning laser needs a direct line of sight to the bar code, and the bar code itself needs to be reasonably clean and undamaged—one reason your cashier might have to swipe that bag of spuds four or five times before the scanner reads it.

Now there's something better—roughly six times better—than bar codes. A very small electric crystal chip can be embedded into products to provide up to ninety-six bits of information. It comes from the Office of Naval Research.

The new radio frequency scanners can read the chip whether they have direct line of sight to it or not. The chips themselves are less than an inch long, with the antenna attached, and only about as thick as a pencil lead; the power source comes from the scanner. The new chips store enough information to uniquely tag just about every manufactured item.

The scanner reads not only the category and model number, but also a serial number for the particular item that bears the tag. The tags can be used for all kinds of marking, supply, tracking, inventory management, and logistical tasks. Checking out of the supermarket is as easy as pushing your cart through the supermarket's door.

A as technology continues to advance, a cashless society is being phased in right before our eyes. The ultimate step will be when a mark is invisibly laser tattooed or a new chip is implanted on the hand or the forehead. There will be no fear of misplace mentor theft of credit or debit cards. The mark's PIN number can never be forgotten since it is permanently on the flesh. When all the technology is in place and all the computers are linked, the mark will be usable worldwide.

Many will invariably ask the tempting question, "When will this all happen? How long?" All it will take to bring about this new economic system is a banking failure. The J.P. Morgan derivative exposure and the massive fraud in corporate America has come on the heels of a stock market bubble burst. We are already well on the way to a massive economic failure.

The Red Sea of Worldwide Debt

It is hard to understand the financial predicament of the United States. The national debt is more than six trillion dollars. The yearly deficit seems to be running in excess of four hundred billion. The interest and the debt continue to accumulate at frightening speed. What this means is either tax increases or inflation.

There is no other solution to this ever-present crisis. Since both inflation and tax increases represent a greater burden on people, the system will eventually fall by its own weight of debt. The world follows the United States, so what is true for America is true for the rest of the world. When America entered the Great Depression in 1929, the whole world followed.

The global drug problem, domestic and Third World debt, terrorism, and strange cosmological problems are all creating the climate for a New Global World Economic System.

The idea of a debit system (as opposed to a credit system) has been here for many years. The American people, without a whimper, have been blindly accepting the phase in. As the system is foisted upon America, some people are reluctant to pay their bills with electronic funds transfer, but they are powerless to fight the trend and the momentum the banking system is gaining.

The Last Fulfillment

The coming World Economic System will be just as the Bible predicted two thousand years ago. It will be a cashless system run by a mark that will be placed on the hand or the forehead.

The mark will be mysteriously run by three sixes, and no one will be able to buy or sell except the one who has taken the mark. Certain destruction will come upon all those who take the mark, for this is the ultimate economic system of the Antichrist and the Beast. Those who resist the mark are the ones who will live like vagabonds. These people will mainly consist of Christians and criminals who refuse to be involved in the system.

These insights should make it clear that we are in the time of the end and that the Antichrist is nearer than ever. This third tool of the False Prophet, a revolutionary economic system, is being phased in, bringing about world economic control. A New World Order demands a New World Economic System.

CHAPTER THIRTY

The King of the World

The final chapter in the conspiracy against God and man will be the attempt of the coming Antichrist to set up the ancient throne of King David in Jerusalem and establish himself as the king or the president of the World.

WHY THE THRONE OF DAVID?

The throne of King David has great eternal significance. Jerusalem, according to the ancient prophets, is to be the theocratic venue of Christ's millennial reign on earth. The forces of evil will attempt to circumvent this plan. Through violence (followed by a false peace), the forces of darkness will set up the "man of lawlessness" (the Antichrist) in place of the rightful heir, Christ Jesus.

The Christian church's anxious longing for the return of Christ will continue until these malevolent events take place. Yet these events must take place before His earthly kingdom can come. Millions of His people do not realize that when He returns, the kingdoms of this world will be finished and His Reign will last for one thousand years. In that reign He will rule with a rod of iron (Revelation 2:27).

Over the centuries, Satan—through his incredible strategy of the Global World Order—has been busily shaping the world for his ultimate control. His desire is, once again, to seat himself in the place of the Most High. Isaiah describes the first attempt to usurp God's throne in heaven, and now Satan will try again for God's throne on earth. The throne of God on the earth is the throne of King David (Isaiah 14:13).

When Christ walked on the earth, the original disciples expected an immediate restoration of the Davidic kingdom. They believed Jesus would immediately establish His rule (see Acts 1). The disciples believed that Jesus was the Son of David and that He would quickly move to restore the glory of David's Kingdom which had been lost for one thousand years (Matthew 9:27). Not only did Old Testament prophecy reveal Jesus as the coming Son of David, but, when He arrived on the scene some two thousand years ago, Jesus clearly responded to that title.

Now, after more than two thousand years since Christ's day, the world is rapidly moving into a Global World System—both political and economic—that is, a counterfeit millennial kingdom. Yet there is no apparent king (Antichrist) to run the show.

Yet, this entire false system should excite the hearts of every Christian; it is a major sign of Christ's return (2 Thessalonians 2:1-12).

To sum up: Jesus is the Son of David who will come to rule the world. He will destroy this Global World System, which will have its initial locus in Western Europe and the United States but will eventually remove to Jerusalem. It will be ruled for a short time by the usurper, Antichrist, who will attempt to lay claim to the ancient throne of David.

WHO IS THE ANTICHRIST?

In the Old Testament, God used types as examples to foreshadow events that occur in the latter years. In the case of the usurper (who will come to take control of the Global World Government), there is an interesting Old Testament type. A careful study of this Old Testament type is important in shedding light and detecting the advance of the Antichrist.

OLD TESTAMENT PARALLEL

The parallel can be found in a story centered around King David at the time when his kingdom was firmly in hand. At that moment in Jewish history, Israel was a unified nation, not divided between north and south. It was at the height of its glory. But even though David's kingdom seemed firmly under control, his immediate family was having some horrific problems.

The underlying reason for the internal discord came from problems that arose out of David's concept of marriage. King David was a polygamist. Though David was a man who loved God and sought after Him more than any other in his day, his desire for many women led to tremendous problems within his own family. It seems strange that God never spoke to him on this matter but allowed him to continue on in this grave error.

There came a time when a serious conflict arose amongst the children of his family. David had many sons and daughters from different wives. The problem arose from David's son Amnon's irresistible lust for David's daughter Tamar (a daughter from a different mother than Amnon). Amnon was so aroused by his half sister that he became psychotically distraught. He sought council from David's nephew Jonadab, a very shrewd man whom Amnon considered a friend. Jonadab counseled Amnon on how to manipulate Tamar into a compromising situation and then take her by force sexually (2 Samuel 13:1-14).

Amnon took this advice, and Tamar was shamed. News of the rape came to Tamar's full-blooded brother Absalom, and, as a result, Absalom deeply hated Amnon. Absalom waited for his father, the king, to deal with the debacle, yet David failed to act in a disciplinary way toward Amnon.

Absalom continued to hold onto his hatred for Amnon. He reasoned that if his father would do nothing, then he would act independently (2 Samuel 13:24-39). After all, the Law of the Jews declared that:

> And if a man shall take his sister, his father's daughter, or
> his mother's daughter...it is a wicked thing; and they
> shall be cut off in the sight of the their people: he hath
> uncovered his sister's nakedness; he shall bear his iniquity.
> *Leviticus 20:17*

When the king delayed disciplining Amnon, Absalom took the Law into his own hands and made arrangements to murder his brother.

After he succeeded, Absalom fled from Jerusalem and his father. He lived in obscurity for several years, but eventually he returned to Jerusalem to once again seek the favor of his father. David, however, shunned his son. Then Absalom, feeling justified and self-righteous about taking Amnon's life, conspired to usurp the throne of his father (2 Samuel 15:1-12).

It is an interesting exercise to speculate on the machinations of Absalom's inner reasoning. Perhaps he felt that his father was too old and couldn't execute sound judgment any longer. After all, didn't the Law require action against Amnon? Or maybe Absalom felt that, underneath it all, his father was really a weak man who couldn't act against his own family with the kind of punishment that the Law required for the crime of rape.

Whatever the reasoning and motivations, Absalom sought to usurp the Davidic throne. Absalom the murderer now became Absalom the thief and usurper. Satan himself is characterized in the New Testament as a liar, a thief, and a murderer. Absalom crosses a line in relationship to the Davidic throne and the holy city of Jerusalem and, thus, inherits the character of Satan. The Antichrist that is to come will have these same attributes; he will cross those same lines.

LUCIFER'S CHARACTER

Satan, as he is revealed in the Bible, was once an archangel. Lucifer's character has not changed; his modus operandi and his hatred toward God is still the same. He formerly desired to usurp God's throne. In Absalom we see the reenactment of that twisted character, and Absalom is an unsuspecting pawn.

Any compromised human agent will do for the purposes of the "prince of the power of the air," as he is called (Ephesians 2:2). David's own son was a prototype of the coming Antichrist.

IMPLICATIONS OF THE ASSAULT

When the Lord Jesus came to the earth initially, He had to fulfill every prophecy spoken of Him. Most specifically, however, He had to be a descendant of the royal line of succession of the kings of Israel. At the same time, He had to be born through immaculate conception by the Holy Spirit.

In other words, He had to be born of the seed of man and the seed of God at the same time. Hence, He would refer to Himself as the Son of Man and also the Son of God. Christ, however, could not have an earthly father; the blood of the human race was tainted with a curse. Life is transmitted by the blood and the sin nature is passed on to each successive generation by the male side of the human race.

Christ, the incarnation of the living God, could not have the sin nature of the human race and still be God (Colossians 2:9). By being of the seed of the woman (through Mary) and yet being immaculately conceived (by the power of the Holy Spirit), God accomplished the task of not only fulfilling prophecy, but setting up the necessary ingredients for the rescue of the human race.

Mary was a descendent of King David through Nathan, David's son through Bathsheba, and therefore in the lineage of the royal King David. Through Mary's ancestry, Jesus obtained the titles of Son of Man and Son of David.

CHRIST'S LEGAL INHERITANCE

Jesus, however, would have had no legal claim to the earthly throne had it not been for Joseph. Joseph, His stepfather, was the key to the legal claim of Christ to the throne of King David. Joseph was a descendant of David, too, only Joseph's line of ancestry proceeded from Solomon, from whom came the royal line of the kings. Therefore, Christ's legal claim to the throne of David came as a result of the marriage of Joseph to Mary before

Jesus was born. This marriage was necessary to enable Christ Jesus to be the legal heir to the throne of David even though Joseph was not the natural father of Jesus.

Furthermore, though Joseph could make the Lord Jesus the legal heir to the throne (1 Kings 9:5,6), Jesus could not be connected to the succession of the actual kings. His humanness had to come from Mary. This was due to another taint that was placed upon the kings at the time of King Jeconiah. This particular king was so evil that God had to literally take back a provision He had made. Jeconiah had transgressed to the degree that God could no longer keep His promise the original way He intended it. The legal rights could be conferred, but the literal seed would not descend. Of Jeconiah God says:

> Write ye this man childless, a man that shall not prosper
> in his days: for no man of his seed shall prosper, sitting
> upon the throne of David, and ruling any more in Judah.
> *Jeremiah 22:30*

Joseph had to have a connection to the royal lineage of Solomon to whom God had made a promise that an heir would be forever seated on his throne. Joseph's genealogy, as it is traced in the book of Matthew, ends with his connection to the royal lineage of King David through Solomon.

One last important thing: Joseph had to be wed to Mary prior to the birth of Jesus to confer this legal right of succession. Had Joseph delayed becoming Mary's husband until after Jesus was born, Jesus would have been illegitimate. By wedding Mary before the birth, Joseph became the legal father of Jesus, imparting to Jesus the legal right to the throne of David (Matthew 1:24).

Had Absalom succeeded, had the conspiracy supplanted King David and his throne, it would have prevented Jesus from coming to the earth. It is conceivable that God could have worked out another virgin birth through some other party. However, that would have made Jesus Christ the Savior and not the coming King.

We see here the operation of the foreknowledge of God and the absolute literal fulfillment of prophecy. God, in His infinite knowledge and wisdom, worked out through time that His Son be not only Savior of the world, but also the heir to the throne of King David.

It must be remembered that Satan's murder of Christ at the hands of the Romans and the Jews was because Christ claimed to be King. Satan seeks a throne and a kingdom, as we have seen. When the throne of David was assailed during David's lifetime (by the adversary through human agency) and then again during Christ's lifetime, it becomes clear that this is Satan's purpose on the earth. He will try again, but this time by seating himself on the throne of a One World Government.

LUCIFER'S CLEAR PATTERN

Lucifer, at one time, was very close to God. He was the anointed cherub. It was through an insurrection that the attempt on God's throne came. It was through an agent whom God trusted and who was given hallowed secrets of the government of God (Isaiah 14:12-14). On earth, in the person of Absalom, the same pattern occurred. A son, who was trusted and deeply loved by his father, turned and sought—through satanic inspiration—the usurpation of the throne.

During the time Jesus walked the earth, the pattern emerged again. This time the traitor was Judas, one of the original disciples (John 13:2,3). The repetition of Satan's behavior makes the pattern clear. The Antichrist will arise from one who has been given great trust and power. It may come from one who is even now considered a Christian, or perhaps someone of Jewish descent. "But in his estate shall he honour the God of forces: and a god whom his fathers knew not" (Daniel 11:38). Certainly this scripture indicates he will come from either of those two camps.

But just as God had Lucifer outflanked before, He still has all things under control. All these events are taking place in order to prove and test the people the Lord God has called unto Himself.

CHAPTER THIRTY-ONE

How Then Shall We Live?

You may be asking, "How shall I live after hearing such a message? What can I do? How should I live out my life? What is my responsibility as a believer, as a disciple, as a citizen of America? What good is all this knowledge? What is God's intent with disclosing all these things to me?" These questions typically flood the mind of the hearer.

The Lord Himself spoke in these apocalyptic terms, but He always pointed towards a positive end for those who believe, the negative signs always coming before His return.

It is the natural man that finds this information fantastic, fatalistic, and unbelievable. "It's so negative! Where is the peace and the hope?" The spiritual man knows that, no matter what happens, the Lord is his confidence. It is the natural man that looks for ease and comfort. He has no place for the consideration of a world that offers trouble and that doesn't offer a real hope for reaching earthly goals. The natural man seeks the peace that the world gives. The spiritual man seeks the peace that comes from above.

> Peace I leave with you, my peace I give unto you: *not as the world giveth*, give I unto you. Let not your heart be troubled, neither let it be afraid.
>
> *John 14:27 (emphasis added)*

In the face of all the external confusion and chaos, God's Spirit steadies our inner man with these promises:

> I will never leave thee, nor forsake thee.
>
> *Hebrews 13:5*

> The LORD is my rock...
>
> *Psalm 18:2*

> For our light affliction, which is but for a moment, worketh for us a far more exceeding and eternal weight of glory; While we look not at the things which are seen, but at the things which are not seen: for the things which are seen are temporal; but the things which are not seen are eternal.
>
> *2 Corinthians 4:17,18*

> And when these things begin to come to pass, then look up, and lift up your heads; for your redemption draweth nigh.
>
> *Luke 21:28*

These manifestations of events coming into view, long ago foretold by the prophets, have been given so that we can discern the nearness of Christ's Second Coming. What can be more encouraging for those who long for His return than to see the fulfillment of biblical prophecy coming to pass? The kingdom is coming! We should be genuinely excited because *the day of the Lord is near.* The signs point to that nearness.

It is only the flesh that gets in the way. The flesh fears the uncertainty of the world and the cataclysmic changes that are coming—and, as with 9/11, the events that have already come. If our hope and peace rest in the stability that the world has to offer, we will suffer great loss and have great fear. The Word of God teaches the disciples to grip the world loosely, not to tighten our hold on that which is failing—for it *will* fail. If ever there were a time when people should be taking to heart the admonition to "love not the world," it is in this hour.

We are on the brink of what Scripture calls perilous times. The One World System is so close that even the most casual glimpse bears witness to this fact. All the saints should seriously reevaluate their relationship with the Lord and get their spiritual house in order. The King is coming!

We must leave dead churches and find churches where the Lord is truly visiting His people. The authentic presence of the Holy Spirit is the critical factor. We must not settle for mere lip service to the Holy Spirit; we mst seek the genuine presence of God. We must be able to touch the Living Hope. If we fail to contact God—or, rather, fail to let Him contact us—then we will look to the world for security and its false peace and hope. The world's answer to man's essential needs is empty. The deceitfulness of sin entices a trust in the world, but there is no real hope in the world. There is only hope—lasting hope—in Jesus Christ.

THE OUTWARD RESPONSE

What about our culture? Should we just give it up and let the current trends take their course?

The message in this book gives new insights into the world where we live. It is a hurting world where God's people are being prepared—and where millions of people still walk in great darkness.

The information in this book was intended to give the panorama of time from a biblical perspective. Those that grope in darkness have no clue. God uses His people as His hands and feet (we are the body of Christ) to do His bidding on the earth. The Church has been reaching out for two thousand years, but we are not finished with our work. We are in the last of the last days.

Consider how many people really are headed into eternal life having accepted the New Covenant. More than likely, it is not as many as we think. That it is why the information that has been given is so vital to those who are lost and staggering about in this twisted world. For Christians, it is a wake-up call to get their priorities in biblical order.

There is tremendous blessing and responsibility for everyone who has read this far. It means fruitful labor and eternal purpose. These insights are weapons for the tearing down of powerful strongholds—strongholds that exist in peoples' minds. These insights must be spoken.

We must remember that "God so loved the world, that He gave his only begotten son" (John 3:16). Christ wants us to fight a good fight. He wants us in the battle. We must also see that the people being used by the devil to bring about a One World Government are loved by the Lord as well. We must raise the standard of Christ in every quarter. Not only as it pertains to peoples' salvation, but also as a preservative for our culture.

In the secular schools, we must stand against a false morality. On the job, we must tell the story to unbelievers of why their taxes are so high and why the deficit is so large. We must tell people who is behind it all and how they can become part of the solution. In government, we must overturn immoral and ungodly laws that break down the structure of the nuclear family and tear at the core of society.

We must battle the gay and lesbian rights movements along with euthanasia and the women's movement, which are all proponents of godlessness. We must get involved in putting an end to the drug problem. Where is the church? We need new troops. We must become more involved in the abortion issue, as many already have. We must be involved in every dimension of civic life. Where are the men to coach Little Leagues and basketball? Where are the mothers for Girl Scouts? We must get involved, so that we can become all things to all men *so that we might win some.*

The people of the world are looking for leadership in every area. God's people must take the responsibility and aspire to fill the positions. After all, who is more qualified? We have the mind of Christ. What are we waiting for? Move ahead and be the answer! Leadership positions will place us in the arena so that we can tell the story of our Leader. There is no hope coming from the world. There is no lasting peace from the world. The answer is not there.

THE MOST CRITICAL FACTORS

The information in this book should make you less inclined to be of this world, but retreating from it is absolutely not God's answer, nor His will. To be in but not of the world does not mean to abandon it and run for the hills. The knowledge that the world is passing away should cause us to act as a preservative until Christ takes us out. *Don't take yourself out before the Lord does.*

The friction that comes from engaging the enemy in this final round of battle is God's plan for the restoration of our souls. We must learn that, as we stand for the Lord and model Christ in the face of Satan, we gain the Lord's character and nature. The battle enables us to become more fashioned like our King. We are perfected by faith in Christ. It is in the heat of battle that we learn to trust in the Lord. This is His end-time plan for the perfecting of the saints. Let us run to the battle line and engage the enemy.

ENGAGING THE ENEMY

It is not enough to fill all the positions of leadership where the lost can be won. Certainly evangelization must continue until the Lord returns, and God's only hope for the lost is the outstretched arm of the church. But we must remember that we are fighting a spiritual war. We must use spiritual weapons for that war. They are essential for our fight. It is at the point of spiritual warfare where there rests a delicate balance; the balance rests on prayer and external effort.

We simply must pray without ceasing. We must first engage the enemy in the spiritual realm. We engage the enemy, then we bind him with the use of the keys to the kingdom. Then—as instructed throughout the whole of the Bible, specifically in the book of Ephesians—we are instructed to put on the whole armor of God.

> Put on the whole armour of God, that ye may be able to stand against the wiles of the devil. For we wrestle not against flesh and blood, but against principalities, against powers, against the rulers of the darkness of this world, against spiritual wickedness in the high places…. Stand therefore, *having your loins girt about with truth*, and *having on the breastplate of righteousness*; And *your feet shod with the preparation of the gospel of peace*; Above all, taking the shield of faith, wherewith ye shall be able to quench all the fiery darts of the wicked. And *take the helmet of salvation, and the sword of the Spirit*, which is the word of God: Praying always with all prayer and supplication in the Spirit, and watching thereunto with all perseverance and supplication for all saints.
>
> Ephesians 6:11,12,14-18 *(emphasis added)*

We must diligently use our authority as sons of God to war against Satan and bind him in the name of Jesus. We must pray to God, model the person of Jesus, and speak the Word.

The plan is this: We must reach up continually to our Father, in all matters, and trust in Him. We must know that the battle is essential so that Christ be fully formed within us. We are called to win the lost. We should not fear this hour in which we live. This is the greatest time to be alive in all the history of the world. Jesus is coming again. The difficulty of these times serves to make us more like Him. Though we lose the world, we gain the Lord.

HIS REWARD IS WITH HIM TO GIVE TO EVERY MAN

Millions of people unknowingly depend on you to take your place, to be ready to give an answer to anyone who asks you the reason of the hope that is in you. "In the world ye shall have tribulation," Jesus said, "but be of good cheer; I have overcome the world" (John 16:33).

The following statement by the prophet Habakkuk sets this whole work into proper perspective. Habakkuk was told by God of the coming day when the Babylonians would be raised up to overwhelm the world and displace Israel. God told him to write the vision down so that it would be very plain to anyone who would read it.

This day is no different than that time, so his words apply. The knowledge of the coming judgment was unbearable to him, but this is what he wrote.

> When I heard, my belly trembled; my lips quivered at the voice: rottenness entered into my bones, and I trembled in myself, that I might rest in the day of trouble: when he cometh up unto the people, he will invade them with his troops. Although the fig tree shall not blossom, neither shall fruit be in the vines; the labour of the olive tree shall fail, and the fields shall yield no meat; the flock shall be cut off from the fold, and there shall be no herd in the stalls. Yet I will rejoice in the LORD, I will joy in the God of my salvation. The LORD God is my strength, and he will make my feet like hinds' feet, and he will make me walk upon mine high places.
>
> *Habakkuk 3:16-19*

Chapter Thirty-two

Summary

This book has shed new light on an old topic. It has laid out the panorama of human history so that the reader can gain greater objectivity with a fresh Christian worldview. It has been shown that throughout time the human race has been moving toward a One World Government, eventually to be ruled by a man who would claim to be the master of the human race: the Antichrist.

Step by step, light has been shed on the world empires and the powerful people that have arisen throughout time and are nudging the master plan along. With the death blow to the British Empire from the great world wars of the twentieth century, the focus of this exposition shifted the spotlight onto the infamous False Prophet.

Since most theologians have been blinded by an incomplete understanding of the False Prophet, the central thesis of this book has been to identify the False Prophet and his two horns as the United States and Great Britain. Also, it made clear that the False Prophet has immense power, which he uses to set up the final system (the Beast) of the Antichrist along with ten kings. The ten kings of the Beast system shall be ruled by the Antichrist and have worldwide impact.

The spiritual purpose underlying this book is to retrieve and reactivate many believers who have succumbed to the temptations of the world and have lost their zeal for the Lord. The high ground of a Christian worldview gives God's perspective on human history, disengages the love of the world, and prepares the heart for the King of kings to rule and reign.

To God be the glory!

Appendix

If the False Prophet is a system how can it be thrown into the lake of fire?

This is a question that is frequently asked by those who have accepted the teaching that the False Prophet is a man. It is easy for the imagination to accept a man being thrown into a lake of fire, since he is an object. However, a system being thrown into the lake of fire is a problem for the human imagination because a system is not tangible.

The importance of the question is an enormous consideration. Let us use an analogy to explain. Have you ever flown in an airplane over the United States? If you have, you obviously noticed that you couldn't tell the difference between, say, California and Arizona. There are no lines separating the states like you would see on a map—and likewise across the whole country. There is only a continuous land mass.

That is because the United States, in actuality, only exists on paper. If there were no state constitutions delineating and designating the borders and the boundary lines, there would only be a known land mass. That is exactly what we see from the plane: the land mass. The United States only exists because men decided there would be a country with individual states. They drew up constitutions and state boundary lines. The United States only exists on paper.

Take the Constitution, the state constitutions, the IRS tax codes, and America's treaties and throw them into a fire. What do you have? The end to the political entity called the United States. Only the land mass is left—with, of course, houses, cars, people, etc., but *no political or economic definitions remaining.*

America only exists, in a sense, in code. If you burn up the codes in a fire, you destroy the political reality. The False Prophet is a symbol that represents a code, the outworking of which produces a political entity.

Before we press on, a computer code is a very strange configuration that derives its creation from keys on a keyboard. When a programmer writes in a code the outworking of that code on a screen, it has absolutely no resemblance to the code itself. This is the same for the codes in Revelation. The symbols of Revelation are *pictorial portals of spiritual codes.*

In this case, the code explains a political reality (America and England). If you throw the symbol (the False Prophet—the code) into the lake of fire (a spiritual fire), you destroy the code. When the code is destroyed, so is the political reality it has produced. The same thing happens if you destroy a computer code that has produced a program. Destroy the code and the program that it has produced vanishes. Ever throw an icon in the trash bin? No more program.

Apart from God, Satan is the master of code creation in the spiritual dimension. Most likely, the tree of the knowledge of good and evil had to do with the invitation to the knowledge and mastery of code.

Consider the phenomena of movie making. When we visit the cinema, we watch a movie on a screen which is the projection of light through a film strip. We hardly ever think of the film strip, but we could not see movie unless there was light being projected through a cellulose film. All we know is that we are seeing an image on a screen.

The real essence of the movie, however, is not what we see on the big screen but the film strip itself. If one were to tear down the thirty-foot screen, it would not bring an end to the film strip. We could go to the movie house down the street and project the same film strip on that screen and—voila!—we could be back in business watching our movie. But take the film strip, throw it in a fire, and burn it up: That is the end of the movie forever.

The False Prophet (a code) is like the film strip that projects on this world the code that it represents: a political system of the two kingdoms (England and the United States). Burn the False Prophet (the code) in fire (the lake of fire) and there is no longer the *political system* (England and the United States). The land mass still remains—and is not destroyed. Only the political entity is destroyed.

Just like every Beast in the Bible represents a kingdom (a political system), the False Prophet is also a political system of two kings. And he is destroyed.

One last note: Many have tried to say that since the word *he* is a personal pronoun, the False Prophet has to be a man. But in Daniel 8, notice that the two beasts identified as Mede-Persia and Greece are also characterized with the personal pronoun *he*. Yet it is cleanly speaking about two nations states represented by beasts. The pronoun *he* does not represent a man; it is a symbol representing animals.

Endnotes

Chapter 1: The Last Stroke

1. Eustace Muffins, *The Secrets of the Federal Reserve* (Stauton, VA: Bankers Research Institute, 1985), 3.
2. Ibid.
3. Hal Lindsey, *Late Great Planet Earth* (Grand Rapids: Zondervan, 1970), 105.

Chapter 7: The Mother of All Harlots

1. The Jewish Encyclopedia, 9:309.
2. Alexander Hislop, *The Two Babylons* (Neptune, NJ: Loizeaux Brothers, 1916), 40-42.
3. Ibid., 75.
4. Ibid.
5. Ibid.
6. R. Woodrow, Babylon Mystery Religion, 153.

Chapter 8: Tracking the Beast

1. Philip Myers, *Ancient History*, Table of Contents. Myers' book is a good example of many historical books that explain the evolution of the great empires.

Chapter 9: Mystery Babylon

1. Hislop, *The Two Babylons*, 41-45.
2. Ibid.
3. Ibid.
4. Ibid., 18-19.
5. Ibid., 12-19.
6. Ibid.
7. Ibid., 20-21.
8. Ibid.
9. Ibid.
10. Ibid. 41-45.
11. Ibid., 30-32.
12. Ibid.
13. Ibid.

Chapter 10: The Five Fallen Kings

1. World Book Encyclopedia (World Book Inc.: 1988), Egypt, 6:133-144.
2. Ibid.
3. Ibid.
4. Ibid.
5. Ibid.
6. Hisiop, *The Two Babylons*, 22.
7. Ibid., 38
8. Myers, *Ancient History*, 62-69.
9. Ibid.
10. Ibid., 38.
11. *New Bible Dictionary* (Grand Rapids: Eerdmans, 1967), 119.
12. Myers, *Ancient History*, 88.
13. Ibid., 93-94.
14. Ibid., 89.
15. John Walvord, *Daniel—The Key to Prophetic Revelation* (Chicago: Moody Press, 1971), 129-131.
16. Myers, *Ancient History*, 90-91.
17. Ibid., 95-97
18. Star, *History of the Ancient World*, 378-385.
19. Hislop, *The Two Babylons*, 49-50.
20. Ibid.
21. Ibid.,48.

Chapter 11: Rome: The Sixth Empire

1. Harper's *Dictionary of Classical Literature*, 1387.
2. Star, *History of the Ancient World*, 575.
3. Ibid., 576.
4. Ibid., 576-600.

Chapter 12: The Seventh Head

1. World Book, Vol. 2, the entire section on England.
2. John Reeves, *The Rothschilds, Financial Rulers of the Nations*, 167.
3. World Book, section on England
4. Ibid.
5. Des Griffin, *Descent into Slavery* (Clackamas, OR: Emissary Publications, 1978), 26-27.
6. Des Griffin, *Fourth Reich of the Rich* (Clackamas, OR: Emissary Publications, 1976), 41-45.
7. Ibid.
8. Anton Chaitkin, *Treason in America* (New York: New Benjamin Franklin House, 1985), 265-304.
9. Ibid.

10. Ibid.
11. Ibid.
12. Ibid.
13. Ibid.
14. Ibid.
15. Ibid.
16. Ibid.
17. Ibid.
18. Ibid.
19. Ibid.
20. Ibid.
21. Ibid.
22. Ibid.
23. Griffin, *Descent into Slavery*, 26.
24. Nesta Webster, *The French Revolution* (Nesta Webster, 1919), 2-36.
25. Ibid.
26. Ibid.
27. Griffin, *Descent into Slavery*, 26.
28. R.E. Epperson, *The Unseen Hand* (Tucson: Publius Press, 1985), 140.
29. Ibid.
30. Ibid.
31. Ibid.
32. Griffin, *Fourth Reich of the Rich*, 88.
33. Epperson, *The Unseen Hand*, 166 & 168.

Chapter 14: World Wars I and II

1. John Robinson, *Proofs of Conspiracy* (Boston: Western Islands, originally published in 1798), 57-156.
2. *Challenging Years*, 189-197.
3. Griffin, *Descent into Slavery*, 95-98.
4. Griffin, *Fourth Reich of the Rich*, 124.
5. Griffin, *Descent into Slavery*, 26-40.
6. Ibid.
7. Ibid.
8. Konrad Heiden, *Der Fuehrer* (Boston: Houghton Mifflin, 1944), 64-65.
9. Ibid., 5.
10. A.S. Sutton, *Wall Street and the Rise of Hitler* (Seal Beach, CA: 76 Press, 1976). The entire book is a record of the banking powers' arming of Hitler.

Chapter 15: The Great Sword

1. Sutton, *Wall Street and the Rise of Hitler*, 67-76.
2. Joseph Carr, *The Twisted Cross* (Shreveport, LA: Huntington House, 1985), 36.

3. Heiden, *Der Fuehrer*, 1-18.

4. Cleon Skousen, *The Naked Capitalist* (Salt Lake City: 1970), 30. Lord Balfour worked within the Round Table's elite, including both Rhodes and Rothschild.

5. Heiden, *Der Fuehrer*, 65.

6. Ibid., 64.

7. Ibid., 528.

8. Ibid., 586-87.

Chapter 16: The Satanic Resurrection

1. Griffin, *Descent into Slavery*, 34-46.

2. Mullins, *The Secrets of the Federal Reserve*, 1-2.

Chapter 18: The False Prophet (the Second Beast)

1. W.E. Vines, *Expository Dictionary of New Testament Words* (London: Oliphant, 1940, Distributed by Revel), 1:222.

2. W.E. Vines, *Expository Dictionary of New Testament Words*, 1:89.

Chapter 19: History of the False Prophet—the New Zion

1. Peter Marshall, *The Light and the Glory* (Old Tappan, NJ: Revell, 1977), 106.

2. Ibid.

3. Ibid., 110-11.

4. Ibid.

5. Ibid.

6. Ibid.

7. Ibid.

8. Ibid.

9. Ibid., 270-309.

10. Charles Noburn, *Honest Money* (Asheville, NC: New Puritan Library, 1983), 8-9.

11. Ibid., 9-11.

12. Ibid.

13. Charles Norburn, *Honest Government* (Asheville, N.C.: New Puritan Library, 1984), 10-11.

14. Norburn, *Honest Money*, 10-11.

15. Ibid.

16. Ibid.

17. Skousen, *Naked Capitalist*, 8-11.

18. Ibid.

19. Ibid.

20. Ibid.

21. Martin Larson, *The Secrets of the Federal Reserve*, 10.

22. Robinson, *Proofs of Conspiracy*, 57-156.

23. Ibid., 58-60.

24. Ibid.

25. Ibid., 58.

26. Ibid.

27. R.E. Epperson, *The New World Order* (Tucson: Publius Press, 1990), 110.

28. Ibid., 84

29. Karl Marx and Frederick Engels, *The Communist Manifesto* (NY: International Publishers, 1948), Point #5,30.

30. Chaitken, *Treason in America*, 53.

31. Ibid., 5-19.

32. Ibid.

33. Ibid.

34. Ibid.

35. Ibid.

36. James D. Horan, *Confederate Agent, A Discovery in History*, 16.

37. William McIlhany II, *Klandestine*, 12.

38. Epperson, *The Unseen Hand*, 155.

39. Abraham Lincoln, speech in Springfield, IL, January 1837.

40. Epperson, *The Unseen Hand*, 160. The Knights of the Golden Circle was the fountainhead of the assassination.

Chapter 20: History of the False Prophet—the Post-Civil War Era

1. G.G. McGreer, *The Conquest of Poverty*, 169.

2. Irwin Ungar, *The Greenback Era, 1865-1869*, 352-3,356-61, 370.

3. Ibid.

4. Alexander Del Mar, *History of Money in America*, 36.

5. Chaitkin, *Treason in America*, 291-304.

6. Ibid.

7. Ibid.

8. Ibid.

9. Ungar, *The Greenback Era*, 352-3, 356-61, 370.

10. Ibid.

11. Norburn, *Honest Money*, 29-35.

12. Griffin, *Fourth Reich of the Rich*, 88.

13. Norburn, *Honest Money*, 33.

14. H.S. Kenan, *The Federal Reserve Bank; the Most Fantastic and Unbelievable Fraud in History* (Los Angeles: The Noontide Press, 1966, rev. 1967), 48.

15. Mullins, *The Secrets of the Federal Reserve*, 16.

16. Robinson, *Proofs of Conspiracy*. George Washington made this famous statement in response to the notion of a central bank controlled by an elite group of men.

17. Constitution of the United States of America. POWERS OF CONGRESS: Article 1, Section 8, Paragraph 5.

Chapter 21: History of the False Prophet—Anglo-Americanism

1. Clarence Kelly, *Conspiracy Against God and Man* (Belmont, MA: Western Islands, 1974). The whole book is a historical record of the conspiracy.
2. Skousen, *The Naked Capitalist*, 27-29.
3. Carroll Quigley, *Tragedy and Hope; A History of the World in Our Times*, 270-268.
4. Ibid., 130.
5. Ibid.
6. Carroll Quigley, *The Anglo-American Establishment* (Books in Focus, 1981), 33-34.
7. Skousen, *The Naked Capitalist*, 31.
8. Ibid.
9. *The World Crisis: The Aftermath*, 147.
10. Quigley, *Tragedy and Hope*, 132-133.
11. Ibid., 951.
12. Lawrence Shoup and William Minter, *The Imperial Brain Trust* (NY: Monthly Review Press, 1977), 1-56.
13. Phoebe Courtney, *The CFR*, 36.
14. Skousen, *The Naked Capitalist*, 31.
15. Ibid.
16. Ibid.
17. The Review of the News, April 9, 1980, 37-38.
18. Skousen, *The Naked Capitalist*, 54.
19. Ibid.
20. Ibid., 54.

Chapter 22: The Two-horned Beast

1. Quigley, *The Anglo-American Establishment*, 3-14.
2. Sheldon Emry, *Billions for Bankers, Debts for the People: How Did it Happen?* (Phoenix: America's Promise Radio, 1967).
3. Ibid.
4. Chaitking, *Treason in America*, 293-295.
5. Griffin, *Descent into Slavery*, 66.
6. Ibid.
7. Kelly, *Conspiracy Against God and Man*, 173.

Chapter 25: The Image of the Beast

1. Vines, *Expository Dictionary of New Testament Words*, 2:243-4.
2. Ibid., 4:325-6.
3. Ibid., 2:337 & 1:149.
4. George Gurben, Annenburg School of Communication.
5. Ibid.
6. TV, The Media, 72-73.

7. Ibid.
8. Ibid.

Chapter 29: Laser Scanning Systems for Supermarket Automation

1. Roger Palmer, *The Bar Code Book* (Heleners Pub. Co., 1989), 11-14. Also, for complete history on bar code, consult *Reading Between the Lines*, by Craig Harmon and Russ Adams (Heleners PuI. Co., 1984).
2. Ibid., 19.
3. Ibid.
4. Ibid.
5. Ibid., 22.
6. Mary Stewart Relfe, *The New Money System* (Montgomery, AL: Ministry Inc., 1981), 54.
7. Ibid., 47-53.

Bibliography

Barnes, H.F. *Pearl Harbor a Quarter Century Later*. Clackamas, OR: Emissary Publications, 1968.

Boer, H.R. *A Short History of the Church*. Grand Rapids: Eerdmans, 1976.

Carr, J.J. *The Twisted Cross*. Shreveport: Huntington House, 1985.

Chaitkin, A. *Treason in America*. NY: New Benjamin Franklin House, 1985.

Commanger, H.S. *Documents of American History*. NY: Appleton, 1949.

Courtney, P., *The CFR*.

Del Mar, A. *History of Money in America*.

DeMoss, A. *The Rebirth of America*, U.S.A.: DeMoss, 1986.

Douglas, J.D. *Red Cocaine*. Atlanta: Clarion House, 1990.

Epperson, R.E. *The New World Order*. Tucson: Publius Press, 1990.

————. *The Unseen Hand*. Tucson: Publius Press, 1985.

Fry, L. *Waters Flowing Eastward*. New Orleans: Flanders Hall, 1988.

Griffin, D. *Fourth Reich of the Rich*. Clackamas, OR: Emissary Publications, 1976.

————. *Descent into Slavery*. Clackamas, OR: Emissary Publications, 1978.

Heiden, C. *Der Fuehrer*. Boston: Houghton Mifflin, 1944.

Hislop, A. *The Two Babylons*. Neptune, NJ: Loizeaux Brothers, 1916.

Horan, James D. *Confederate Agent; A Discovery in History*.

Hunt, D. *Peace, Prosperity and the Coming Holocaust*. Eugene, OR: Harvest House, 1983.

Kelly, C. *Conspiracy Against God and Man*. Belmont, MA: Western Islands, 1974.

Kenan, H.S. *The Federal Reserve Bank; the Most Fantastic and Unbelievable Fraud in History*. Los Angeles: The Noontide Press, 1966 (rev. 1967).

Larson, M. *The Federal Reserve*.

Lindsey, H. *The Late Great Planet Earth*. Grand Rapids: Zondervan, 1970.

McGreer, G.G. *The Conquest of Poverty*.

McIlhany, William. *Klandestine*.

Marrs, T. *Millennium*. Austin, TX: Living Truth Publishers, 1990.

Marshall, P. *The Light and the Glory*, Old Tappan, NJ: Fleming H. Revell, 1977.

Marx, K. and Engels, F. *The Communist Manifesto*. NY: International Publishers, 1948.

Mullins, E. *The Secrets of the Federal Reserve*. Stauton, VA: Bankers Research Institute, 1985.

Myers, P. *Ancient History*.

New American Standard Bible, Open Bible Edition. Camden, NJ: Nelson, 1979.

Norburn, C.S. *Honest Money*. Ashville, NC: New Puritan Library, 1983.

————. *Honest Government*. Ashville, NC: New Puritan Library, 1984.

Palmer, R. *The Bar Code Book*. Helmers Pub., 1989.

Pike, W.P. *Israel: Our Duty, Our Dilemma*. Clackamas, OR: Emissary Publications, 1984.

Quigley, C. *The Anglo-American Establishment*. Books in Focus, 1981.

————. *Tragedy and Hope: A History of the World in Our Times*.

Reeves, J. *The Rothschilds: Financial Rulers of the Nations*.

Relfe, M.S. *The New Money System*.

Robertson, P. *The New World Order*. Word, 1991.

Robinson, J. *Proofs of a Conspiracy*. Boston: Western Islands.

Roebuck, C. *The World of Ancient Times*. 1966.

Shoup, L. and Minter, W. *The Imperial Brain Trust*. NY: Monthly Review Press, 1977.

Skousen, C. *The Naked Capitalist*. Salt Lake City: 1970.

Star, R. *History of the Ancient World*. NY: Oxford Press, 1974.

Stewart, M. *New Money or None*.

Stormer, J. *None Dare Call it Treason*. Florissant, Missouri Liberty Bell Press, 1964.

Sutton, A.S. *Wall Street and the Rise of Hitler*. Seal Beach, CA: 76 Press, 1976.

Ungar, I. *The Greenback Era, 1865-1869*.

Walvord, J. *The Rapture Question*. Grand Rapids: Zondervan, 1976.

————. *Daniel—The Key to Prophetic Revelation*. Chicago: Moody Press, 1971.

Walvord, J. *The Revelation of Jesus Christ*. Chicago: Moody Press, 1966.

Webster, N. *Surrender of an Empire*. London: Emissary Publications, 1931.

————. *The French Revolution*. N. Webster, 1919.

Woodrow, R. *Babylon Mystery Religion*. 1966.

Index

About the Author

Ken Klein is a Hebrew Christian and has been a believer for more than 34 years. Ken Klein was born in Los Angeles California in 1946. He was raised in the Jewish Religion and converted to Christianity in 1969. He has been married to Jan Klein for 29 years and has three children: Jonathan, 26; Michael, 25; and Daniel, 20.

At the age of 18 Ken moved to Oregon where he starred as defensive halfback for the University of Oregon football team, and later graduated with a B.S. degree in social sciences.

After college he made his way into the National Football League where he played briefly with both San Francisco Forty-niners in 1967 and the Houston Oilers in 1968.

He has pastored three churches, authored several books and has produced ten films. He has appeared on thousands of radio and television talk shows including appearances with almost every major Christian broadcaster in the United States.

He currently is executive director of Ken Klein Productions, a Christian film production company. He has produced many video documentaries on the end times, and his current films include: *Temple Mount Dilemma, Petra—Israel's Secret Hiding Place,* and *Twenty-five Messianic Signs.* The blockbuster films of *Cracking the Prophetic Code* (the United States in Prophecy) and *In the Shadow of Babylon* are in hot demand.

On the following pages are short cameos of those films.

Mr. Klein can be contacted via e-mail at:
stromwarn@aol.com

Please feel free to visit the web site at:
www.kenkleinproduction.com

Petra

Israel's Secret Hiding Place

Dr. Noah W. Hutchings &
Ken Klein

Founded in 2000 B.C., this ancient city Petra holds an extremely significant place not only in world history, but also in the prophetic future.

Founded by Esau (the twin brother of Jacob whose name later was changed to Israel), Petra became the most fabulous city of the Edomites, and a prominent world trading center before, during, and after the time of Christ.

Though it has been a ghost town for more than one thousand years, according to the Jewish prophets, Petra figures to be the future hiding place of Israel during the later half of what is commonly called the great tribulation.

Literally carved out of the red rock sandstone in the mountains of Jordan, this ancient home of Esau was the stronghold and fortress of the Edomites, the implacable foe of Israel. Learn today who are the current and modern remnant of the Edomites.

In the Shadow of Babylon

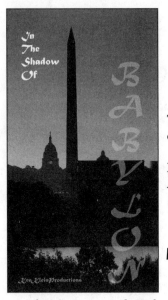

Order Now

Throughout time the human race has been tormented by an unseen religious dynamic. This unrelenting power has deceived the nations raining down on the inhabitants of earth as an almost perfect storm. The Scripture calls it Mystery Babylon, and it is characterized in the apocalypse, in symbolic form, as the "Great Harlot."

This powerful imposing force impersonated herself as truth as she subtly poses in the name of righteousness, thus deceiving the unwary. It is the mother of all religions, and the power that fragments even the Church of our Lord. It is Mystery Babylon.

She pours out her wine and the nations have become drunk with her deception, but still she goes unnoticed. Even the massive sectarianism of Christendom bears witness to the religious power, as she injects the venom from the snake that she is.

Who is she, where is she, and how has she deceived the nations? Do we all lay in the "Shadow of Babylon"? From this video comes the ultimate revelation of the source of all religious confusion, not only in the obvious cults, but also in the more subtle tones of Christianity.

See how pagan Babylon has infected the world's religions, the Moslems, the Jews, and the Church throughout time even to the door of your own church.

The whole world lies in the power of the evil one. *In the Shadow of Babylon* casts a floodlight on this darkness, dispelling the confusion (for Babylon means confusion).

25
Messianic Signs

Order Now

In the ancient ages the great Hebrew prophets from Israel predicted that before the coming of their promised Messiah...there would come specific signs, or what would amount to the fulfillment of their prophesies, that would signal the end of the AGE...

Over each successive millennium the peoples throughout the world have wondered, pondering exactly when those times would come—looking forward and trying, were it possible, to hasten those days.

Not until the Jews returned to the Land in 1948 could those signs become evident, and clearly seen...Today, some 50 years after being back in the land, those signs become patently clear even to the casual observer.

From the mountains flowing with sweet wine, to the wars of the Jews with the Moslem nations, to the rebuilding of the third Jewish temple, and much more, you will experience and see it all as *Twenty-five Messianic Signs* brings to you the unfolding drama of the appearance of the Prophets signs—signs that point us to the unparalleled and greatest moment and event of all time...the Return of Messiah.

Join Dr. Noah Hutchings and Ken Klein as they tour the "Holy Land" reporting on the most amazing fulfillment of Biblical Prophecy in our time—right from the exact locations where they have occurred.

To Order

Videos

1.	Temple Mount Dilemma	$14.95	_____
2.	Twenty-five Messianic Signs in Israel	$19.95	_____
3.	Petra—Israel's Secret Hiding Place	$19.95	_____
4.	In the Shadow of Babylon	$19.95	_____
5.	Cracking the Prophetic Code	$19.95	_____
6.	Israel Islam & Armageddon	$19.95	_____
7.	Art Katz's—The Mystery of Israel	$14.95	_____
8.	Art Katz's—The Time of Jacob's Trouble	$14.95	_____
9.	Art Katz's—The Mystery of God	$14.95	_____

Book

America, Globalism, and the False Prophet $14.95   _____

Please add $5.95 for individual orders and
only $6.95 for multiples   Total   _____

Send to:
Ken Klein Productions
P.O. Box 40922
Eugene, OR 97404
e-mail: stromwarn@aol.com

For wholesale distributor rates on books or videos please call: 1-800-888-1363

Please visit our web site at: www.kenkleinproductions.com

For wholesale distribution call 1-800-888-1363